CHARBNEAU SO-CALLED DOLLARS

Jeff Shevlin
William D. Hyder

Discover the World of

Charbneau So-Called Dollars

From the 1939-40 Golden Gate International Exposition

An Illustrated Reference

To Wild Bill,

Jeff Shevlin

So-Called Books

Published by:
So-Called Books
7737 Fair Oaks Blvd., Suite 250
Carmichael, California 95608

http://So-CalledDollar.com/

ISBN 978-0-578-08559-3

Printed in the USA by
Signature Book Printing
www.sbpbooks.com

Disclaimer: No warranty or representation of any kind is made concerning the accuracy or completeness of the information presented, or its usefulness in numismatic purchases or sales. The opinions of others may vary. The authors may buy, sell, and sometimes hold certain of the items discussed in this book.

TABLE OF CONTENTS

Special Dedication	vii
Preface	ix
San Francisco's Golden Gate International Exposition	1
Jules Louis Charbneau	13
Charbneau So-Called Dollars	23
1939 Gold So-Called Dollars	29
1939 Silver So-Called Dollars	41
1939 Copper So-Called Dollars	49
1940 Gold So-Called Dollars	55
1940 Silver So-Called Dollars	61
New Directions in Research	65
Bibliography	69
Acknowledgements	71
About the Authors	73

Special Dedication

Although there are many individuals worthy of recognition for the contributions they have made to this book, there is one person who stands out amongst others. That person has shared my numismatic adventures and journeys, reveled with me when rare pieces were acquired and shared my joy when research pays off and new discoveries are made. After looking at a new find she hands the medal back to me and says "that's nice."

No, she is not a numismatist, she is not even a coin collector, but she has fueled my passion for numismatics for over 35 years, my wife Cecilia Shevlin.

Jeff Shevlin
11/21/2009 San Carlos, Mexico

Preface

For over 70 years numismatists have known the name Jules Charbneau was connected with the souvenir item called the "Gold Dollar" issued for the 1939-40 San Francisco Golden Gate International Exposition. The Gold Dollar—actually a tiny medal—was engraved by an enigmatic "CMJ." The chore of researching this medal, the people connected with it, its importance, history and varieties, has been embraced by the two authors whose detailed results are revealed here in this work. Can they put some flesh and blood to and identify who was the mysterious Jules Charbneau? Can they identify who was CMJ?

The increasing popularity among collectors of so-called dollars, led in no small part by the lead author of this work, has brought a heightened interest in all so-called dollar issues. It is of benefit to numismatists, to expo enthusiasts, and perhaps even to San Francisco historians, to learn more about the gentleman whose name has been associated with this medal for seven decades.

Gold dollar-sized medals were included among the list of so-called dollars by the pioneer cataloger of this topical medal series, Richard D. Kenney (1918-1957); his premier list of so-called dollars was published in the Wayte Raymond periodical, *The Coin Collector's Journal* (July-August 1953). Jules Charbneau (1883-1968) was identified with his Gold Dollar in the medal title in the 1963 standard work on the subject, compiled by those giants of the topic, who gave their names to the HK catalog numbering system, Harold E. Hibler (1904-1968) and Charles V. Kappen (1910-1999).

Both of these publications gave rise to more questions than they answered, but brought into focus the scope of this collecting topic. The authors of both publications did try to define exactly what is a "so-called dollar." Everyone who collects these pieces inherently knows what they are—souvenir medals nearly the same size as the U.S. silver dollar, or the one-dollar gold piece, as is the case of the Charbneau Gold Dollar. Richard Kenney was strict in his definition of these pieces, while Hibler and Kappen expanded the circle, being a little more liberal, by listing eight criteria in which they placed a medal in this class of collectibles.

The size is one of convenience. The one-and-one-half inch size of a silver dollar is that of a large coin or a small medal, at this intersection of the two numismatic forms. For early makers of these pieces—particularly those struck by the U.S. Mint—the convenience was having on hand existing blanking dies to create the blanks or planchets to strike these pieces in bronze or silver.

This was, of course, before the vast popularity of the vending machines, as in the 1920s, when that industry's complaints increased because slugs, the exact size of U.S. coins, were ending up in their vending machines, turnstiles, fare boxes, parking meters and public telephones.

While no collector would ever place one of his beloved so-called dollars in a vending machine, this industry outcry did lead to a rash of state and national Slug Laws in America. These were codified in the U.S. Code (Title 18, Part 1, Chapter 25, Section 491).

The existence of such laws, however, did give concern to medal issuers of possibly violating any of these laws by making their medals the exact size of a silver dollar. In one instance—on the other side of the continent from the 1939 San Francisco Expo, at the 1939 New York World's Fair—the Manufacturers Trust Company wanted a silver-dollar size medal to honor that fair.

The bank's solution was to order the shape changed from round to oval in fear of those Slug Laws. The so-called dollar, HK 491, modeled by sculptor Henry Kreis (1899-1963), was struck by Medallic Art Company in a reeded oval medal as one of the most unusual pieces in the series.

Without the restrictions of a Slug Law, Jules Charbneau proceeded to issue his Gold Dollars. He had been inspired in this venture by that of numismatist Farran Zerbe (1871-1949) at the 1904 St Louis World's Fair, in which Charbneau had attended with his bride on their honeymoon. Zerbe was active in promoting the Lewis and Clark gold dollars. Perhaps Charbneau remembered this 35 years later.

For the motif of his 1939 Gold Dollar, Charbneau took the facial image of a mammoth eighty-foot tall statue, a tribute to the entire Pacific area, the Ocean and the nations that surround it. Pacifica dominated the entranceway to the Expo grounds, with a "mysterious countenance" as described by the authors.

It was a most extreme case of contrasts. Jules Charbneau was a practitioner and collector of miniature objects, he had a large collection of his miniatures on view at the Expo. Yet he chose as the device for his Gold Dollar the face of that mammoth statue, towering over every entrant to the Expo. Pacifica reigned supreme from on high in contrast to the tray of tiny gold discs on sale for a few dollars at Charbneau's stall adjacent to his exhibition of carved miniatures.

This is a delightful story about the artist, the event, and the highly collectible little numismatic items. Call them "dollars," or call them "medals," you are extremely fortunate if you own even one of Charbneau's creations. The book is highly illustrated with associated items, the post cards, the prints and pictures, the map and posters, the covers, tickets and programs, the related expo items, all of which add luster to the little gems, known as Charbneau's Gold Dollars.

D. WAYNE JOHNSON
Corporate Historian,
Medallic Art Company

Overleaf: Collage based on the Charbneau dollar and Si Vanderlaan's design for the cover of the 1939 Official Guide Book, Golden Gate International Exposition.

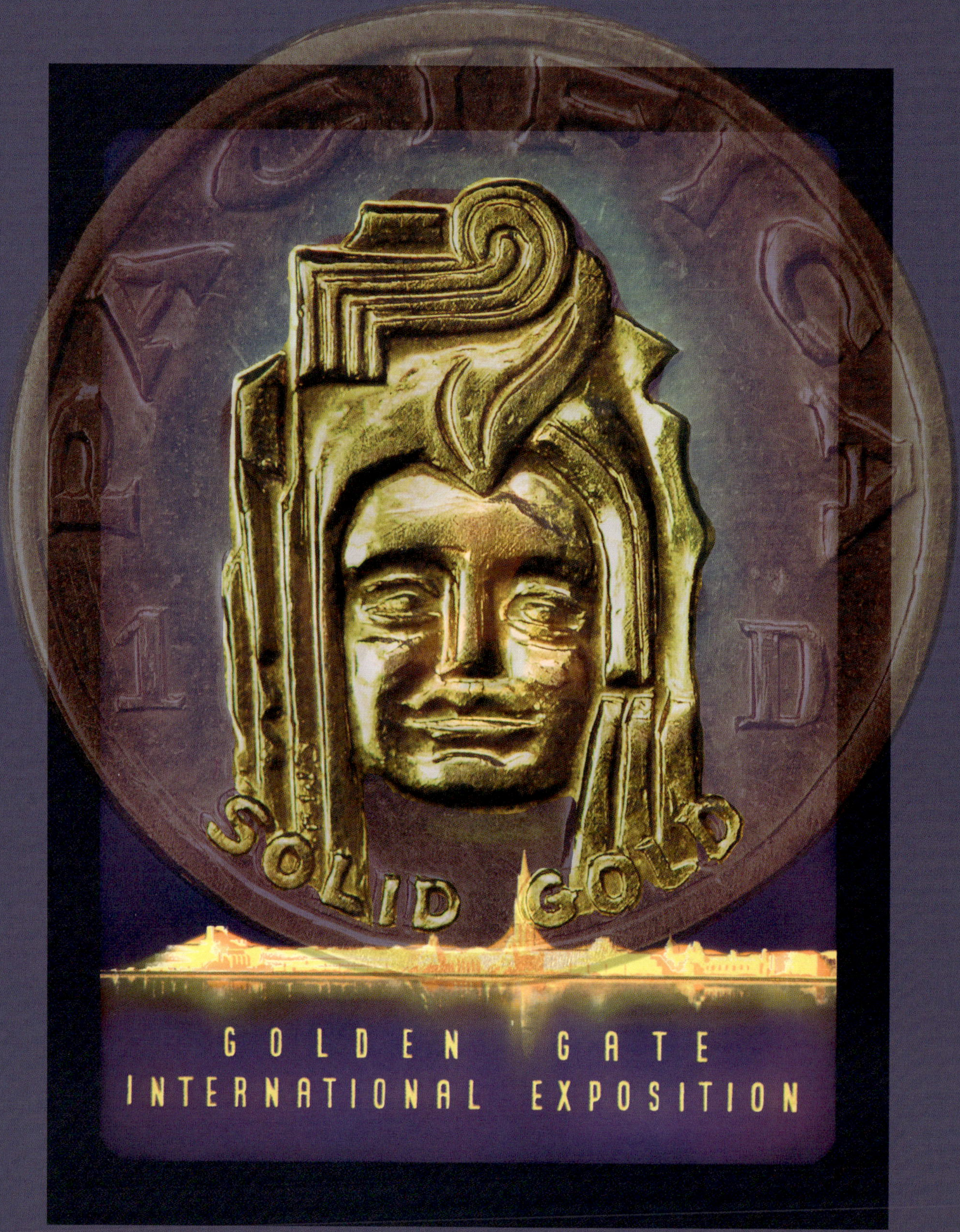
SOLID GOLD
GOLDEN GATE
INTERNATIONAL EXPOSITION

SAN FRANCISCO'S GOLDEN GATE INTERNATIONAL EXPOSITION

Pacifica smiling? Visitors to San Francisco's Golden Gate International Exposition sometimes stood before Ralph Stackpole's eighty-foot personification of the exposition theme, Pacifica, waiting for her calm, contemplative and enigmatic expression to break into a smile. Some said they had seen it happen, others were not so sure. Regardless of what they think they saw, a stop at Jules Charbneau's Miniature Curiosities afforded the visitor an opportunity to carry home a small token with her visage to contemplate at their leisure. To this day, Charbneau's gold "dollars" continue to perplex and fascinate coin collectors and connoisseurs of world's fair memorabilia.

The Golden Gate International Exposition—the Pageant of the Pacific—opened to the public on February 18, 1939 amidst worldwide unease over the belligerent behavior of Germany and Japan. Civilian, as well as military, casualties were mounting in the undeclared Sino-Japanese War, but the Japanese carefully avoided a declaration of war to avoid drawing the United States into the conflict. Hitler's Germany annexed Austria, embraced state-sponsored persecution of the Jews, and was on the verge of invading Czechoslovakia, yet appeasement remained the official policy of European democracies. In the United States, people were still struggling to overcome the devastating effects of the Great Depression.

Pacifica's mysterious countenance reflected the American psyche as San Francisco opened the gates to her third international exposition. It was not the world envisioned in 1933 when San Francisco embraced the idea of celebrating its progress on completion

The Charbneau Dollar reflects the "Pacifica" style that distinguished exposition architecture. Gold, 12mm.

of the two majestic bridges then under construction.

Grand world fairs showcasing the ingenuity, innovation, and productivity of the Industrial Revolution had become economic revival engines for cities and regions struggling with prolonged economic doldrums. San Francisco experienced the economic benefits of expositions in 1894 and 1915. Why not mount

GOLDEN GATE BRIDGE

SAN FRANCISCO-OAKLAND BAY BRIDGE

a third exposition to revitalize the city and its bay area neighbors once again? The Golden Gate Bridge and the San Francisco-Oakland Bay Bridge promised to open a new chapter in the history of San Francisco. Construction was underway despite the economic depression and completing the bridges would be cause for a grand celebration.

A Bridge Celebration Founding Committee first met on October 10, 1933 to lay the foundation for the fair. Architects W. P. Day and George W. Kelham accepted an assignment to evaluate potential sites. They eliminated Golden Gate Park from consideration, as the required destructive physical changes to the landscape were no longer compatible with land management policies. China Basin and Candle Stick Point offered good transportation access, but the industrial settings were far from attractive. The Marina district, site of the Panama-Pacific International Exposition, had developed extensive residential and recreational uses incompatible with exposition requirements, although its location on the bay was consistent with the planned bridge celebrations.

Yerba Buena Island would connect the east and west spans of the Bay Bridge and it afforded a clear view of the Golden Gate. The U.S. Navy used the island for training and navigation aids, including a lighthouse. The Yerba Buena Shoals to the northwest had long presented a hazard to shipping. On closer investigation, the hazardous nature of the shoals could be turned to an advantage for exposition planners. The location in the shadow of one bridge provided an open

Above: Treasure Island as seen from the Yerba Buena causeway. The Administration Building and one of the two permanent hangers are clearly represented along with the Elephant Towers that formed the Portals of the Pacific framing the Tower of the Sun. The Court of Pacifica can be distinguished at the top end of the island near the approaching ship. The legend, Made in Japan, is tucked into the rim along the lower rim. The reverse depicts the two bridges without the presence of Treasure Island. Chrome-plated tin, 72mm.

Opposite Page, Top: The Golden Gate Bridge emerges from the fog, while the Bay Bridge and Treasure Island are visible in the upper right corner of the photograph.
Opposite Page, Bottom: The San Francisco - Oakland Bay Bridge crosses Yerba Buena Island as it spans the bay. Treasure Island estends to the left of Yerba Buena Island in the middle of the bay.

The completion of the Golden Gate and the San Francisco-Oakland Bay Bridges prompted calls for a world's fair to celebrate the achievement. A variety of exposition souvenirs such as the one overlaid on the two images were produced to commemorate the bridges and the Exposition. Brass, 32mm.

Promotional events to raise funds for the exposition began early in the project. The publicity committee produced a variety of items such as the Magic City "stamp" gummed to attach to envelopes. The Treasure Island theme was further promoted by a group of twenty-five "Buccaneer Girls" led by the twenty-one year old Fern Arnold.

water view of the other, plus it would be readily visible from the San Francisco waterfront.

San Francisco had already incorporated the shoals into the city limits based on an earlier proposal to fill them for the construction of an airport. Those plans created the basis for selecting the exposition site. Rather than a frivolous effort for a short-term event, site preparation could be funded via the aviation efforts, an important consideration given the expense of building an artificial island in the middle of the bay.

Construction of the island began in 1936. The U.S. Army Corp of Engineers oversaw construction efforts funded by the Works Progress Administration (WPA) as eleven dredges pumped sand from bay navigation channels to fill the shoal. Approximately 287,000 tons of rock was placed to form a seawall nearly three miles long to enclose the emerging 400-acre island. Later, 10,000 pilings were driven into the rocky bottom to create a foundation for the exposition buildings.

As the island began to emerge from the bay, it was dubbed Treasure Island, the name inspired by the adventure book written by the one time San Francisco resident, Robert Louis Stevenson. The publicity committee introduced Miss Fern Arnold as the Buccaneer Hostess dressed in red satin shorts, a green blouse, orange sash, and black pirate hat in keeping with the swashbuckling theme.

A causeway linked Treasure Island to Yerba Buena Island and the Bay Bridge. Loam from the Sacramento River delta and fertilizer was added to create soil. WPA funding provided for 1,200 staff to plant the thousands of trees, shrubs, grasses, and millions of flowering plants needed to complete the landscaping planned for the site.

Federal funding also underwrote the construction of three permanent exposition structures: the two buildings designed to become future airport hangers and the main passenger terminal and control tower. Pan-American Airways moved into the terminal when it was completed having earlier launched its "clipper ship" passenger service to the Orient in anticipation of a permanent base of operations at Treasure Island.

The architectural design for world fairs often provided the lasting images for which the fairs were remembered even though the buildings were usually temporary. Since the site was meant to become an airport at the close of the fair, the three permanent buildings had to be incorporated into the plans. The future airport control tower topped the four story, horseshoe-shaped administration building situated adjacent to the causeway entry gate at the island's southwest corner. The two permanent hangers completed the southern edge of the island. The unique architectural focus was reserved for the center of the island aligned along an approximate east-west axis.

The architectural committee proposed a new style they dubbed "Pacifica." George W. Kelham, drawing on his experience designing the master plan for the Panama-Pacific International Exposition (P.P.I.E.), chaired the committee until his death in 1936. Arthur Brown, Jr. succeeded Kelham. Brown is known for the San Francisco City Hall and Coit Tower as well as portions of Stanford University and the University of California, Berkeley. Kelham designed a number of public buildings including the old San Francisco Public Library and the San Francisco Federal Reserve Bank. His larger projects included supervising architect and chief planner for the University of California, Berkeley and Los Angeles in addition to his work on the P.P.I.E.

The official emblem, designed by Arthur Brown, Jr., appears on the obverse of the Treasure Island so-called dollar. The small inscription, D–110016, that appears at 6 o'clock refers to Brown's Design Patent. The reverse depicts the China Clipper circling Treasure Island with the sun setting beyond the Golden Gate. White Metal, 33mm.

The architects sought to embody building motifs from the eastern and western shores of the Pacific while softening the impact of massive walls through the use of grand courts. The Portals of the Pacific led to the Court of Honor with the Tower of the Sun, while the grand Northwest Passage ended at the Court of Pacifica. The ramparts of the Portals of the Pacific were modeled after the design of the Mayan

Vintage "Pictorial Wonderland" G.G.I.E. postcard depicting the Tower of the Sun lit at night. The reverse text reads in part, "Four Hundred feet high,—illuminated in amber, shading into a blazing white toward the pinnacle, this spire competes in stature with the towers of the two Greatest Bridges in the world."

Pyramids and topped by stylized elephants to invoke a theme inspired by Angkor Wat. The two themes continued throughout the interior courts to create the impression of an immense walled city.

Arthur Brown, Jr.'s Tower of the Sun served as the focal point for the exposition grounds and the golden phoenix atop its peak, symbolizing the rise of San Francisco from the ashes of 1906, was visible from Oakland and San Francisco. Statues by William G. Huff depicting "Industry," "Agriculture," "Science," and "The Arts" stood in the tower's arches. San Francisco's Grace Cathedral loaned a carillon of 44 bells for the duration of the exposition. Electro-pneumatic hammers rang the bells, driven by paper rolls, a keyboard located in the base of the Tower, or by the simple flip of a switch. The Tower was flooded with white light from projectors concealed in the walls while the Elephant Towers flanking the Portals of the Pacific were bathed in rose red spotlights.

The tower design drew the scorn of local artists. Otis Oldfield from the

Upper Image: Vintage G.G.I.E. "Official Post Card" depicting the eighty foor tall Pacifica standing "before a scintillating metal curtain above the entrance to the Cavalcade of the Golden West and overlooking the Court of the Seven Seas." Lower Image: Souvenir entry ticket showing Pacifica to the left in her Court.

California School of Fine Arts said, "The thing sticks up like the Ferry Building tower. It would have been better if they had a grain elevator in its place." Ralph Stackpole, the artist who created the Pacifica statue that stood in the shadow of the tower was more philosophical. "The thing is up. What can you do about it?" Exposition chief director, Harris Connick, responded to the critics, "It's beautiful, inspiring, impressive—gorgeous by day or night."

The Court of the Seven Seas ran a thousand feet to the northwest from the Tower of the Sun and the Court of Honor ending at the Court of Pacifica. Designed by Timothy L. Pflueger, the Court of Pacifica emphasized Peace. Ralph Stackpole's eighty-foot sculpture, Pacifica, towered over the court. A shimmering metal "prayer curtain" hung as a backdrop, singing as it fluttered in the breeze coming off the bay. Pacifica bemused many art critiques, but they likely held their tongues owing to Stackpole's stature in the San Francisco art community.

Color transformed Treasure Island into the Magic City glimmering on the bay at night. Stucco walls flecked with iridescent vermiculite glowed when illuminated with hidden floodlights and pink, blue, gold, and green fluorescent tubes and "black light" lamps. Graded light intensity from the base to the top of buildings maintained the depths and texture of the architectural elements. The Tower of the Sun rose from the sea of lights to uniquely identify the source of the vision floating on the bay. Pacifica required

Vintage San Francisco Bay Exposition postcard showing the exposition grounds illuminated at night. The four hundred foot Tower of the Sun rises from the Court of Honor with Pacifica standing in her court in the distance.

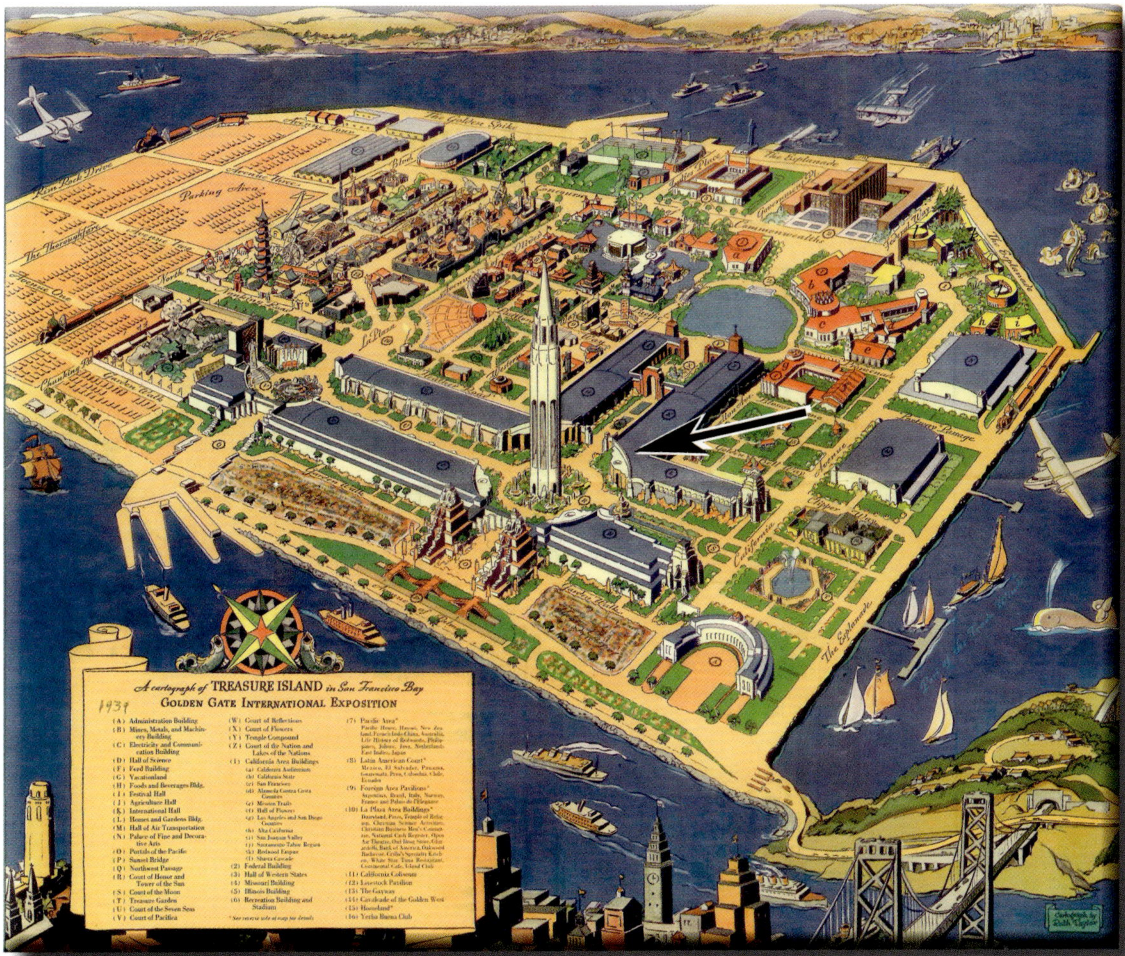

The Exposition map from the 1939 Guidebook as drawn by Ruth Taylor. The large black arrow points to the approximate location of Jules Charbneau's concession, Miniature Curiosities.

a more intimate viewing, bathed in white light at night while the curtain was washed with orange and blue light. Water cascaded from the base and flowed into the central fountain as hidden lights changed its color through a rainbow of hues.

Jules Charbneau operated a concession, Miniature Curiosities, located in the International Hall adjacent to the Homes and Gardens exhibits just a few steps from the Court of Honor and the Tower of the Sun. As a concessionaire, he paid for his exhibit space and presumably charged an admission fee in addition to selling his souvenir gold medals. His long involvement with expositions and fairs undoubtedly guided his choice of these two iconic symbols of the G.G.I.E.—the Tower of the Sun and Pacifica—as the subjects for his gold souvenir token.

Miniature Curiosities seemed perfect for an exposition that featured miniature displays in a number of exhibits. The Atchison, Topeka & Santa Fe Railroad Company relied on a miniature railroad to show the details of its operations from switches and crossovers to water tanks and station houses. The Southern Pacific Company exhibit included the "Little Theater of the West" showing western attractions and Mexican rooms in detail using miniature furniture and bric-a-brac collected from artisans around Mexico. A one-hundred home miniature village displayed the range of housing available in California. The miniature rooms designed and built by Mrs. James Ward Thorne

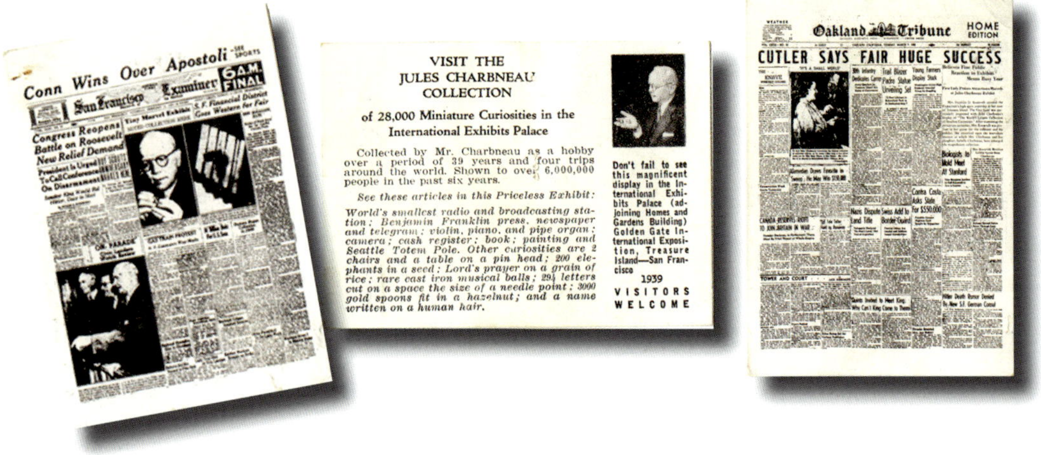

Charbneau distributed miniature newspaper pages with an advertisement for his Miniature Curiosities concession at the G.G.I.E. (Images courtesy the California Historical Society. Ephemera, SF-GGIE-Exhibits-Gen'l)

of Chicago occupied a special section of the Decorative Arts exhibits. Each room portrayed a historic period of design in exquisite detail. The University of California offered a miniature cyclotron that allowed visitors to smash their own atoms. At the other end of the scale, one could check the attendance count displayed on a six-story reproduction of a cash register.

Numismatics, exonumia, and stamp collecting each played a role in the exposition. Phil Shuman ran a California Gold Coins concession. Despite the 1934 Gold Reserve act, one could still collect gold coins, jewelry, and non-bullion items. Bernard Davis offered the Penny Crushers. Novelty shops, souvenir stands, and even a trick card and coin concessionaire allowed one to acquire a number of different tokens and medals commemorating a visit to the fair. The Stamp Clubs of Northern California mounted the "Unique Stamp Collection" on the Gayway and in 1940, all collectors had the opportunity to mount their own displays at the National Hobby Show on the exposition grounds.

Pacifica appears over an aerial view of Treasure Island on a "Good For" advertising token issued by Milens Jewelers of Oakland. Brass, 31.5mm

Unlike many other expositions, it appears the exposition company did not itself issue a commemorative medal. Instead, the concessions department licensed a number of "official" souvenirs, many of which carry seemingly cryptic numbers that register their official nature, although not all items in fact carry their official registration number. Bay area businesses sold Treasure Island pocket pieces for twenty-five cents in 1939. By the summer of 1940, some retailers offered souvenirs for a penny. Several exhibitors gave away or sold souvenir medals and others used the fair to promote their business with tokens redeemable on purchases in their stores. A few of these items are illustrated here. Jules L. Charbneau, however, was responsible for the most mysterious and elusive souvenir, his tiny "gold dollars."

Expositions by their nature are meant to be temporary constructions on the landscape; few if any buildings remain when the gates are closed unless they were planned for future use such as the terminal building and the two aviation hangers. Ralph Stackpole, among others, wanted to see his Pacifica sculpture re-created in a more permanent form somewhere in San Francisco. The threat of war that hung over the Exposition in 1939 became a reality in 1940 and the public's attention turned to more pressing matters.

San Francisco Chronicle columnist, Herb Caen, reported that Charbneau purchased the Pacifica Statue on December 20, 1940 and wanted to move it to a museum he planned to build to house his World of Miniatures. One can image the 80-foot tall Pacifica towering over the two chairs and table sitting on the head of a pin in Charbneau's gallery! We do not know if Charbneau had any idea as to how to move a statute of that size constructed from temporary materials. We do know that the Navy laid claim to the island on April 1, 1941 as necessary for the war effort. They toppled Pacifica with dynamite charges on January 22, 1942, just a few days following Congressional approval of the transfer of the island to the Navy.

The graceful span of the San Francisco - Oakland Bay Bridge and Brown's Tower of the Sun inspired Brown's official logo for the exposition. Details depicted on the Tower of the Sun distinguish this large medal from the general lack of detail apparent in the varieties of the official seal as shown on the obverse of the medal and many other souvenirs. Unlike the medal pictured on page 3, this medal is marked, MADE IN U.S.A., below the tower. Zinc, 62mm

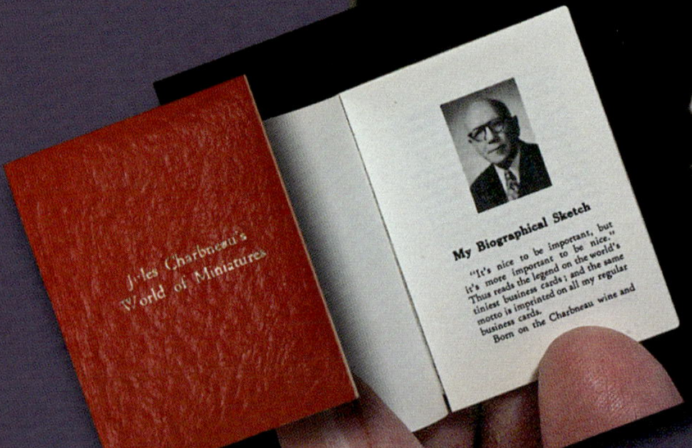

Jules Charbneau related his biography in his own miniature book published in 1968, the year he passed away. In the upper image based on a publicity photograph published in the December 1940 issue of Popular Mechanics, Charbneau examines an item from his miniature Japanese ivory collection.

Jules Louis Charbneau

We found Jules Charbneau a difficult man to trace. His name is often misspelled, even when he supplies the copy for event programs. The problem seems to be the unusual "bn" combination, but Jules and Julius are equally problematic. We know he was born Julius Louis Charbeneau on October 20, 1883 to John C. Charbeneau, a fruit farmer in Mount Clemens, Michigan. His mother, the former Laura Jacques, was born in France although we do not know when she immigrated to the United States.

Mount Clemens was a destination for those seeking the healing power of mineral springs, but was otherwise a small farming community that Julius shared with many probable cousins and other distant relations. We know nothing of his life as a child, but either his mother instilled a desire to travel or he had an intellectual curiosity that could not be met in a small town. For whatever reason, he ran away to New York at age 14 to visit an aunt and spent three months studying and absorbing all he could at the Cooper Union with frequent visits to the Museum of Natural History and the Metropolitan Galleries.

One can only image the thirst of a young boy seeking to learn in an environment heavily influenced by the world of art. Instead of returning home to Michigan, he made his way to Baltimore where he became the mascot for the 1898 Baltimore Orioles, a baseball team with a reputation for taking no prisoners. The Orioles finished in second place that year with one of the best records in their history. Baseball players became his family and the young Julius was the guest of several Baltimore players all in their early twenties living out their own boyhood dreams and adventures.

The Spanish-American War prompted Charbneau to apprentice himself to the

US Navy training ship USS Monongahela.

One can only image the impact the 1900 Paris Exposition had on the young Julius Charbneau. (Neurdein photograph of the 1900 Paris Exposition grounds.)

U.S. Navy. He appears in the 1900 census records for the Newport, Rhode Island Naval Training Station as Julius Louis Charbneau. His apprentice voyage on the USS Monongahela took him to Paris, his first real international experience with the rapidly evolving world of art. The 1900 Paris Exposition Universelle, heavily influenced by the height of the Art Nouveau movement, had another distinct impact on Julius. He purchased a small medal, a miniature jeweled bird, and a miniature meerschaum pipe.

Charbneau's interests and ambitions led to more than art. His intellectual capacity and personal drive earned him the Navy's Bailey Gold Medal as the outstanding apprentice seaman. He out scored and out performed his apprentice class in all skills required to master a naval man-of-war from knots to swordsmanship to mastering the broadside gun and ships accounts. Obedience, industry, and conduct were exemplary as was his personal appearance. His award ensured his assignment to the USS New York, flagship of the Asiatic Fleet, and that experience exposed him to the ports, art, and cultures of the Pacific.

His tour of duty ended in 1904 while in port in Seattle, Washington. One can imagine the young Charbneau discovering the waterfront business, Ye Olde Curiosity Shop, run by Joseph E. Standley. The shop was filled with wonders from the natives of the Northwest Coast and curiosities from around the world as well as many items for sale that undoubtedly interested the young sailor. Fortunately for Charbneau, the shop had just moved to the docks, otherwise he might not have seen it and his life could have taken a far different direction.

Standley's daughter, Carolyn, was likely behind the sales counter. Whatever transpired between the two, Julius took his leave from the Navy and married Carolyn on his birthday, October 20, 1904. The young man obviously impressed Carolyn's parents for they not only employed him in their

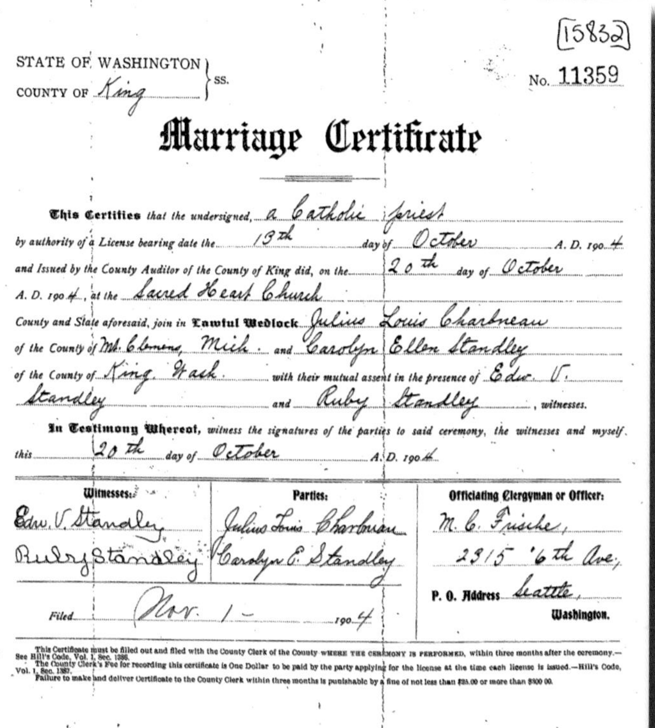

[15832]

STATE OF WASHINGTON }
COUNTY OF King } SS.

No. 11359

Marriage Certificate

This Certifies that the undersigned, a Catholic priest by authority of a License bearing date the 13th day of October A. D. 1904 and Issued by the County Auditor of the County of King did, on the 20th day of October A. D. 1904, at the Sacred Heart Church County and State aforesaid, join in **Lawful Wedlock** Julius Louis Charbneau of the County of Mt. Clemens, Mich. and Carolyn Ellen Standley of the County of King, Wash. with their mutual assent in the presence of Edw. V. Standley and Ruby Standley, witnesses.

In Testimony Whereof, witness the signatures of the parties to said ceremony, the witnesses and myself, this 20th day of October A. D. 1904.

Witnesses:	Parties:	Officiating Clergyman or Officer:
Edw. V. Standley	Julius Louis Charbneau	M. C. Frische,
Ruby Standley	Carolyn E. Standley	2315 6th Ave,
		P. O. Address Seattle, Washington.

Filed Nov. 1 — 1904

This Certificate must be filled out and filed with the County Clerk of the County WHERE THE CEREMONY IS PERFORMED, within three months after the ceremony.—See Hill's Code, Vol. 1, Sec. 1386.
The County Clerk's Fee for recording this certificate is One Dollar to be paid by the party applying for the license at the time each license is issued.—Hill's Code, Vol. 1, Sec. 1387.
Failure to make and deliver Certificate to the County Clerk within three months is punishable by a fine of not less than $25.00 or more than $100.00.

A copy of Charbneau's marriage certificate from Seattle.

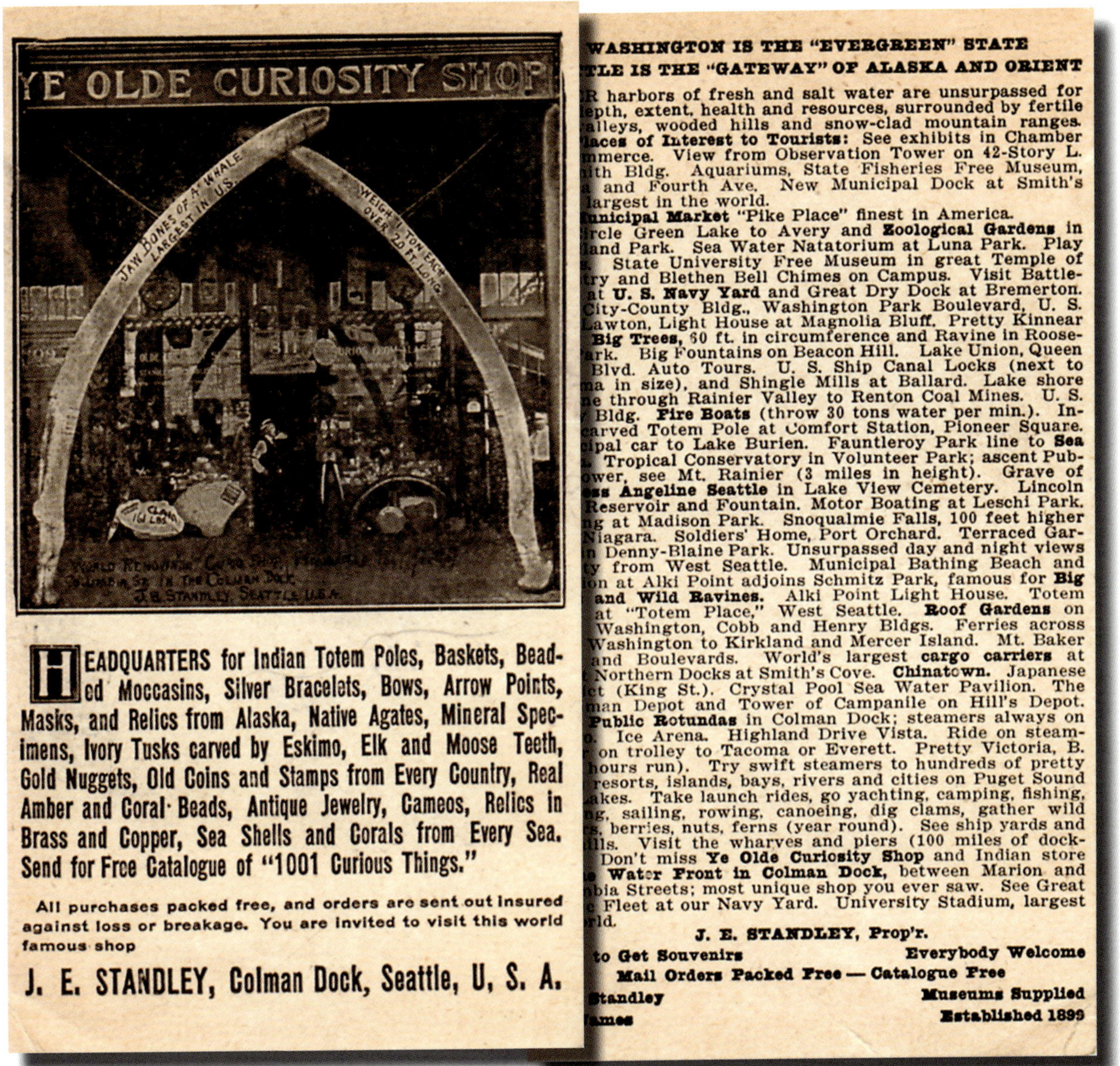

YE OLDE CURIOSITY SHOP

HEADQUARTERS for Indian Totem Poles, Baskets, Beaded Moccasins, Silver Bracelets, Bows, Arrow Points, Masks, and Relics from Alaska, Native Agates, Mineral Specimens, Ivory Tusks carved by Eskimo, Elk and Moose Teeth, Gold Nuggets, Old Coins and Stamps from Every Country, Real Amber and Coral Beads, Antique Jewelry, Cameos, Relics in Brass and Copper, Sea Shells and Corals from Every Sea. Send for Free Catalogue of "1001 Curious Things."

All purchases packed free, and orders are sent out insured against loss or breakage. You are invited to visit this world famous shop

J. E. STANDLEY, Colman Dock, Seattle, U. S. A.

WASHINGTON IS THE "EVERGREEN" STATE
TLE IS THE "GATEWAY" OF ALASKA AND ORIENT

R harbors of fresh and salt water are unsurpassed for epth, extent, health and resources, surrounded by fertile alleys, wooded hills and snow-clad mountain ranges. laces of Interest to Tourists: See exhibits in Chamber mmerce. View from Observation Tower on 42-Story L. ith Bldg. Aquariums, State Fisheries Free Museum, a and Fourth Ave. New Municipal Dock at Smith's largest in the world. unicipal Market "Pike Place" finest in America. ircle Green Lake to Avery and Zoological Gardens in land Park. Sea Water Natatorium at Luna Park. Play s. State University Free Museum in great Temple of try and Blethen Bell Chimes on Campus. Visit Battleat U. S. Navy Yard and Great Dry Dock at Bremerton. City-County Bldg., Washington Park Boulevard, U. S. Lawton, Light House at Magnolia Bluff. Pretty Kinnear Big Trees, 50 ft. in circumference and Ravine in Rooseark. Big Fountains on Beacon Hill. Lake Union, Queen Blvd. Auto Tours. U. S. Ship Canal Locks (next to ma in size), and Shingle Mills at Ballard. Lake shore ne through Rainier Valley to Renton Coal Mines. U. S. Bldg. Fire Boats (throw 30 tons water per min.). Incarved Totem Pole at Comfort Station, Pioneer Square. cipal car to Lake Burien. Fauntleroy Park line to Sea Tropical Conservatory in Volunteer Park; ascent Pubower, see Mt. Rainier (3 miles in height). Grave of ess Angeline Seattle in Lake View Cemetery. Lincoln Reservoir and Fountain. Motor Boating at Leschi Park. ng at Madison Park. Snoqualmie Falls, 100 feet higher Niagara. Soldiers' Home, Port Orchard. Terraced Garn Denny-Blaine Park. Unsurpassed day and night views y from West Seattle. Municipal Bathing Beach and on at Alki Point adjoins Schmitz Park, famous for Big and Wild Ravines. Alki Point Light House. Totem at "Totem Place," West Seattle. Roof Gardens on Washington, Cobb and Henry Bldgs. Ferries across Washington to Kirkland and Mercer Island. Mt. Baker and Boulevards. World's largest cargo carriers at Northern Docks at Smith's Cove. Chinatown. Japanese et (King St.). Crystal Pool Sea Water Pavilion. The man Depot and Tower of Campanile on Hill's Depot. Public Rotundas in Colman Dock; steamers always on Ice Arena. Highland Drive Vista. Ride on steamon trolley to Tacoma or Everett. Pretty Victoria, B. hours run). Try swift steamers to hundreds of pretty resorts, islands, bays, rivers and cities on Puget Sound akes. Take launch rides, go yachting, camping, fishing, ng, sailing, rowing, canoeing, dig clams, gather wild s, berries, nuts, ferns (year round). See ship yards and ills. Visit the wharves and piers (100 miles of dockDon't miss Ye Olde Curiosity Shop and Indian store Water Front in Colman Dock, between Marion and bia Streets; most unique shop you ever saw. See Great Fleet at our Navy Yard. University Stadium, largest rld.

J. E. STANDLEY, Prop'r.

to Get Souvenirs — Everybody Welcome
Mail Orders Packed Free — Catalogue Free
Standley — Museums Supplied
ames — Established 1899

Advertising card (ca. 1917) for J. E. Standley's Ye Olde Curiosity Shop. The shop had much the same appearance in 1904 (the whale bone jaws were laying down and totem poles stood on either side of the shop doors). Is it any wonder that the young Charbneau found it irresistable and fell in love with the owner's daughter.

store, they sent the newlyweds to St. Louis to honeymoon at the 1904 world's fair.

We do not know everything that might have caught Charbneau's eye in St. Louis, but we do know that Farran Zerbe was promoting the sale of the government's commemorative gold dollars and his own "fifty-cent" and "quarter" gold pieces at the Mint's Souvenir Coin Department. Zerbe promoted the gold pieces as tokens implying monetary value, and he sold them in sets of three with the U.S. commemorative gold dollars. Given their small size and

Farran Zerbe produced small fractional gold tokens to sell alongside the U.S. commemorative gold dollars that he marketed and sold at the exposition. Gold, 11.5mm

UNITED STATES PATENT OFFICE.

JULIUS L. CHARBNEAU, OF SEATTLE, WASHINGTON.

DESIGN FOR A MEDAL OR EMBLEM.

No 39,866. **Specification for Design.** **Patented March 9, 1909.**

Application filed January 22, 1909. Serial No. 473,783. Term of patent 3½ years.

To all whom it may concern:

Be it known that I, JULIUS L. CHARBNEAU, residing at Seattle, in the county of King and State of Washington, United States of America, have invented a new, original, and ornamental Design for a Medal or Emblem, of which the following is a specification, reference being had to the accompanying drawing, forming part thereof.

In the drawing, Figure 1 shows the obverse face of the medal or emblem, and Fig. 2 the reverse face thereof.

I claim—

The ornamental design for a medal or emblem, as shown.

JULIUS L. CHARBNEAU.

Witnesses:
N. L. MILLAR,
C. P. SWEET.

DESIGN.

J. L. CHARBNEAU.

MEDAL OR EMBLEM.

APPLICATION FILED JAN. 22, 1909.

39,866. **Patented Mar. 9, 1909.**

Above and Right: The U.S. Design Patent issued to Julius L. Charbneau. Below: The Seattle Star February 13, 1909 article about the novel pure Alaskan gold souvenirs designed by Charbneau for the Alaska-Yukon-Pacific Exposition and Charbneau's efforts to promote the exposition from the Ye Olde Curiosity Shop.

FIGURE ONE FIGURE TWO.

Julius L. Charbneau
INVENTOR.

BY
ATTORNEY.

THE STAR—SATURDAY, FEBRUARY 13, 1909.

HE MAKES PRETTY A.-Y.-P. SOUVENIR GOLD COINS

ARE MINTED OUT OF PURE ALASKA GOLD AND ARE PRETTILY DESIGNED.

One of the most novel souvenirs that have been designed for the coming A.-Y.-P. exposition is the little coin made of pure Alaska gold, stamped with the above designs, representing 1-dwt., or $1 of gold.

There are three coins in the set, the largest being the $1 piece, the next being the ½-dwt., or the 50-cent piece, and the other the ¼-dwt., the 25-cent piece.

The coins were designed by J. L. Charbneau, manager of "Ye Olde Curiosity Shop," on the Colman dock, who has applied for a patent on them. They have been accepted by the exposition officials as the official souvenir coins, and are in great demand for ornaments, such as stick pins, spangles and charms. Coin collectors are enthusiastic about them. Being of real Alaska gold their value as an exposition trophy can not be equalled.

The Alaska-Yukon-Pacific Exposition Gold Piece. Designed by J. L. Charbneau.

Mr. Charbneau is one of the biggest boosters in the city for the A.-Y.-P. and has probably done more than any other private individual in the city to promote its interests, having given out over 10,000 circulars to people leaving the city, or wishing to send them east.

Every caller at the little shop on the Colman dock hears A.-Y.-P. the first thing he enters and the last thing before leaving.

Charbneau's earlier purchase of a small medal in Paris, one might imagine that Zerbe's efforts caught his attention.

Farran Zerbe marketed U.S. gold dollars in 1905 at Portland's Lewis and Clark Centennial Exposition and likely produced the half and quarter Mt. Hood fractional gold pieces to accompany the commemorative U.S. gold dollars once again. It would not surprise us to learn that Charbneau attended the exposition and made note of Zerbe's small gold pieces. His later career paralleled that of Zerbe's in many ways, except Charbneau travelled the country exhibiting his World of Miniatures collection while Zerbe toured with his own World of Money exhibit.

Charbneau settled into life in Seattle managing his father-in-law's shop on the Seattle waterfront Colman Dock. The store specialized in Northwest ethnographic arts and artifacts as well as everything odd or unusual. Jules likely honed his marketing skills and quickly learned to value items purchased for resale. He certainly took interest in the planning efforts for the Alaska–Yukon–Pacific Exposition. With no plans forthcoming for a commemorative dollar, Charbneau proceeded with his own design efforts and applied to the United States Patent Office on January 22, 1909 for a design patent for a new medal made of Alaskan gold.

Charbneau's Pennyweight gold souvenir produced for the 1909 Alaska Yukon Pacific Exposition. Three tokens in the denomination of 1, 1/2, and 1/4 DWT were sold in crimson boxes stamped with the official exposition seal.

The obverse design depicts a standing miner holding a pick over his right shoulder with his left hand on his hip. A shovel and gold pan are visible lying on the ground behind his legs. ALASKA GOLD appears above and A.Y.P.E. below with the date 19 to the left and 09 to the right of the miner. The medal has a beaded border with a plain edge. It was struck in 10K gold in three sizes, 1 DWT, ½ DWT and ¼ DWT. A DWT (pennyweight) is a term used for weighing precious metals and is equal to 24 grains or 1/20th of a troy ounce, approximately 1.55 grams. The 1 DWT is the size of the large US gold dollar.

The February 13, 1909 issue of the Seattle *Star* identified Mr. Charbneau as one of the biggest exposition boosters in the city. The *Star* credited Charbneau with distributing more than 10,000 promotional brochures, ensuring that everyone who entered the Ye Olde Curiosity Shop on the Colman Dock left talking about the coming exposition. Exposition officials accepted his three-coin set made from Alaskan gold as official souvenir coins. The *Star* reported they were already in great demand with enthusiastic coin collectors as well as being sought as charms and ornaments for stick pins.

Standley's ad in the Alaska-Yukon-Pacific Exposition Official Guide. He notes the shop's location for the Offical Gold Coins and his exhibit in the Alaska Building.

Although the Alaska Gold/A.Y.P.E. medals have long been attributed to M. E. Hart of San Francisco, there is no doubt that

An original set of Charbneau's Alaska-Yukon-Pacific-Exposition gold pieces in their box as issued.

they originated with Charbneau through his association with his father-in-law.

Standley influenced and nurtured Charbneau's enthusiasm for Seattle. Ye Olde Curiosity Shop heavily promoted Seattle and its environs and Standley's knowledge of Northwestern native art attracted the attention of anthropologists and collectors alike. His personal collection of Alaskan native art, in particular ivory carvings, was featured in the A.Y.P.E. Alaska Building and received a gold medal. Standley later sold the collection to George Heye, founder of the Museum of the American Indian in New York.

Another Standley son-in-law became active in the business in 1912, so we assume this was about the time when Julius became the curator for the newly formed collection of the Washington State Art Association. The financially troubled young organization merged with the competing Seattle Fine Arts Society in 1917 and Charbneau embarked on his next profession, selling insurance. Between 1920 and 1928, Julius was a leading producer for the Pacific Mutual Life Insurance Company. In 1930, he became one of the founders of Seattle's Washington Athletic Club demonstrating his continued involvement in the city's civic affairs.

The Great Depression had a disastrous effect on the insurance industry. Charbneau turned to lessons learned working in his father-in-law's shop and took his own collection of miniature curiosities on the road. He also became an art appraiser using the skills learned in the shop and the Seattle art community. Businesses booked his collection as an attraction and he displayed it at exhibitions and fairs as a concessionaire charging admission. His costs would have been minimal. The collection required only two trunks to move and his wife, Carolyn, managed the packing and unpacking. Together, they made three trips around the world displaying their collection; adding to it as the opportunities arose.

Helen Cooke discovered the "small, baldish man in a white suit" and wrote about her encounter in the July 24, 1937 *New Yorker* column, The Talk of the Town. New York's Rockefeller Center opened in 1933 and began looking for attractions to draw crowds to the complex of commercial ventures and entertainment. Rockefeller partnered with the Radio Corporation of America, parent company of NBC Radio and RKO Studios, to build Radio City Music Hall. Its Grand Lounge featured revolving exhibitions to keep visitors coming back for "free" entertainment on the chance they would buy theater tickets or shop in the Center stores. It was in the Grand Lounge that Helen Cooke interviewed the man who now called himself Jules.

Cooke's interview tells us that Charbneau began touring with his collection about 1932. While he was thinking of settling down and building a museum, he intended to return to New York and exhibit at the 1939 New York World's Fair. Why did he change his mind and settle in San Francisco and participate in its competing world's fair instead? We suspect the court-ordered 1936 reorganization of the California-based Pacific Mutual Life created new opportunities for the former salesman when the company's outstanding life insurance policies were converted to mutual equity in the company. We also suspect that when Jules moved to San Francisco, he became an independent appraiser contracted to Pacific Life as opposed to full-time company employee.

We do learn something of his travels through the press coverage of his collection. The Emir of Transjordan gave him a camel, small enough to pass through the eye of a needle, as part of a miniature ivory zoo. Charbneau dropped a willi-willi seed containing thirty-six infinitesimal ivory elephants while showing it to the president of

Radio City Music Hall Program for the week beginning Thursday, July 22, 1937. The big screen featured the new RKO-Radio Pictures release, "The Toast of New York," starring Edward Arnold, Carey Grant, Jack Oakie, and Seattle's own Frances Farmer. Seattle's Jules Charbneau exhibited his "world-famous collection of smallest curiosities." Jules likely autographed the program using the same fountain pen as appears in the photograph.

the Coptic Museum in Egypt. Fortunately, Charbneau had his two-inch vacuum cleaner and all but three of the tiny elements were recovered from the deep pile of the room's Oriental rug. In 1936, he took his exhibit to the Japanese Blossom Festival where it was displayed in one of the finest hotels. On another occasion, he met Cardinal Pacelli and commissioned two miniature portraits shortly before the cardinal was named Pope Pius XII. But 1939 found him in San Francisco displaying his miniature curiosities at the Golden Gate International Exposition.

Oakland Tribune reporter, Jack Burroughs, made the G.G.I.E. his personal beat. Burroughs wrote about a small man who made repeated visits to Charbneau's "world's largest collection of smallest curiosities." The small gold spoons—a half a dozen of them could fit in the suit pocket of Charbneau's dressed fleas—mesmerized the man. A week later, Jules Charbneau presented one of the spoons to the first lady, Eleanor Roosevelt, as she toured the fair and stopped to examine his exhibit. He added a gift for the President, a size 28 fishing hook from Oslo, Norway in recognition of the President's prowess as a fisherman. "I hope the President will be able to see it," Mrs. Roosevelt remarked in accepting the gift. As for the little man who fascinated Burroughs, he kept returning because the exhibit "makes me feel so important."

Charbneau signed many of the boxes containing his Pacifica medals.

Burroughs was wary of being accused of accepting kickbacks to promote Charbneau's exhibit, but he assured readers that Charbneau had assured him that it was the largest of its kind. We learn through him and others that Charbneau commissioned many of the pieces in his collection and demanded absolute accuracy in the tiny reproductions of his miniature items. His working desktop radio received its broadcast from an equally small working broadcasting station. Together, they fit in his jacket pocket. Similarly functional were his miniature stove and refrigerator, complete with cooking implements, bowls, and dinnerware. Burroughs was sure a visitor stumped Charbneau when he asked why the tiny bronze rooster did not crow. Charbneau replied that it was a practical model, but it was not supposed to crow because it was "a model of one of those rare deaf and dumb Malay roosters."

It was Burroughs who related the story of trying to catch Pacifica in a smile. He never managed to do so himself, but he did receive a small gold dollar from Charbneau, despite his protestations that he was not on the take! As he stood trying to catch the illusive expression, Charbneau stepped up and slipped him one of the small dollars. Despite rotating the dollar in the light, Burroughs could not catch her smiling, even with the aid of a magnifying glass. He asked about the cryptic "1 D" and Charbneau replied that his medal contained the same amount of gold as a U.S. gold dollar. Burroughs remarked that he could remember when a dollar looked as

Isabella Charbneau Warren plays the miniature grand piano displayed with a variety of her father's other fully functional items including the stove, refrigerator, and the working Ford engine. His miniature business card sits on the desk blotter along with miniature wrting implements. (Seattle Center advertising card.)

"big as the head of a brass drum, but this was the first time a dollar looked as small as the head of a 10-penny nail."

October 20, 1939 was Jules Charbneau Day at the G.G.I.E. in honor of his birthday and his 35th wedding anniversary. His daughter, Isabella, was working with him by this time as an appraiser with her own interests in the collection. Charbneau renewed his concession for the 1940 run of the exposition, and then we lose track of him for a few years. Undoubtedly, the intervention of war and all that followed impacted his exhibitions, but the Cold War opened the opportunity for a new line of business.

As newsreels rolled on May 1, 1954, Jules Charbneau, Chairman of the Board of the Western States Atomic Vaults, formally opened the firm's vault built in an abandoned railroad tunnel near Santa Cruz, California. His collection of miniatures was the first item to be securely stored in the vault, safe from the threats of nuclear war. Later, Isabella exhibited his collection at the 1962 Seattle World's Fair, a homecoming even he could not resist.

His collection eventually came to rest in an exhibit at the Seattle Center from 1963 to 1966 after a side-trip to Tokyo. Jules Charbneau published his own autobiography appropriately in a miniature book, *Jules Charbneau's World of Miniatures*, printed in Japan in 1968. *Miniature Book News* made special note of a "midget folio about midget folios." Jules pasted away in Napa, California on February 28, 1968.

Charbneau's form of performance art—travelling the country to entertain the masses—had all but passed with the post-war economic expansion. Charbneau's daughter, Isabella Charbneau Warren, worked alongside her father and later managed the collection as Jules Charbneau's World of Miniatures museum. She sold items from the collection to a variety of collectors, donated another portion to the North Central Washington Museum in Wenatchee, Washington, and sold the remainder of the collection in 1972 to Ripley's Believe It Or Not.

PACIFICA
1
D
SOLID GOLD
PACIFICA
1
10K
SOLID GOLD
PACIFICA
STERLING
GOLDEN GATE INT. EXPO
1939
PACIFICA
PACIFICA
STERLING
GOLDEN GATE INT. EXPOS
40
1939
GOLDEN GATE INT. EXPOSITION
1940

Charbneau So-Called Dollars

Of the nearly 100 different historical souvenir medals produced for the Golden Gate International Exposition, the tiny and enigmatic Charbneau So-Called Dollars are among the rarest and most valuable.

Over the years a myriad of bits and pieces of information regarding Charbneau dollar varieties has been published resulting in conflicting descriptions and opinions as to what was struck and what exists today. Hibler and Kappen in their book, *So-Called Dollars,* list several varieties, but not all are clearly defined. Burnie in his book on *Small California and Territorial Gold Coins* lists the largest number of varieties, some of which cannot be confirmed and likely do not exist. After many years of extensive research, thirteen distinct varieties have been positively identified and are summarized here. We use a new numbering convention, J1 through J13, to clearly differentiate our catalog types from previous efforts.

Jules Charbneau, a fine art appraiser, dealer, and jewelry designer from San Francisco exhibited his collection of 25,000 miniature hand-carved items at the Golden Gate International Exposition. He also had struck and sold one-dollar sized gold, silver, and copper Charbneau Dollars to commemorate the GGIE, their diminutive size complimenting his exhibit theme.

Hibler and Kappen report that 2,752 total medals were struck including two in platinum, 2500 in gold, 200 in sterling, and 50 in copper. We have not encountered any report of an actual platinum piece. Hibler and Kappen also report that gold pieces were sold for $5 and silver and copper pieces for $1. While we cannot confirm those prices, Charbneau did advertise gold pieces for $3 and silver for 75 cents in 1940 issues of *Popular Mechanics*.

OFFICIAL Gold souvenir coin. Golden Gate International Exposition. San Francisco. Send $3 money order to Jules Charbneau, 645 Stockton St., San Francisco, Calif. Silver coin 75c.

The medals are dated 1939 and 1940, corresponding to the two separate runs of the fair, the first from February 18, 1939 through October 29, 1939 and the second from May 25, 1940 through September 29, 1940. Charbneau dollars are typically described with the dated side as the obverse and the Pacifica head as the reverse. In practice there is little consistency in how one identifies the obverse or reverse of any medal or coin in the absence of an "official" designation by the issuing authority or designer. We prefer to call a head a head and thus Pacifica is the defining element in our opinion. Charbneau's own fascination with Pacifica leads us to believe that he would concur with our choice.

The obverse features the bust of Pacifica, a frontal portrait of the head of Stackpole's 80 foot tall statue Pacifica, "Queen of the Fair". PACIFICA appears in large letters above the bust and along the upper perimeter. Various devices appear to the left, right, and below the bust of Pacifica. The cover of the 1939 GGIE *Official Guide Book* also featured the bust of Pacifica, as did Charbneau's dollars. The reverse is a distinct variation of the official seal with the prominent Tower of Sun edifice and a bridge in the distance. The design adds a ship on the bay and a Clipper airplane in the sky. The inscription, GOLDEN GATE INT. EXPOSITION, arches around the upper half of the rim with the initials CMJ on the left below GOLDEN. The date 1939 appears at 6 o'clock. The profile of the Bay Bridge, a ship and a flying Clipper airplane complete the theme of modern transportation linking the peoples of the Pacific Basin.

When Charbneau was selling his gold dollar sized souvenirs at the G.G.I.E., he had no idea how popular these medals would become years later. Unfortunately for Charbneau, sales were disappointing and it is believed that the majority of the gold, silver, and copper pieces struck were melted.

There are a number of motivating factors that indicate the logical sequence in which Jules Charbneau likely produced his souvenir medals for sale at the GGIE. The first variety produced, J1, is dated 1939 and has SOLID GOLD below the bust of Pacifica with a 1 to the left and a D to the right. Just 12 mm in diameter, it is slightly smaller than a U.S. one gold dollar and the 1 D indicated the value of one dollar. Charbneau also referred to these as one dollar coins. The J1 variety is the most common of the gold varieties with an estimated 20-40 surviving examples. The reverse is dated 1939 below the Tower of the Sun building. They weigh from 1.21 to 1.22 grams and were all struck with a coin orientation. They were not, however, solid gold as indicated but were actually 10K, so Charbneau created a new die by adding 10K above the legend SOLID GOLD (J2). 10K Solid Gold—an interesting oxymoron as solid gold is 24K,

not 10K. Presumably, Charbneau made the 10K correction as a result of his customer inquiries regarding the actual gold content; however, it was not unusual at that time to use the term solid gold for 10K gold content. Considerably rarer the J2 variety is tough to find with perhaps 5-10 examples remaining. The J2 comes with both a coin and medal orientation.

The question of gold content was just the beginning of Charbneau's worries as it was reported he received a visit from the United States Treasury Department concerning his private issuance of money. His medals were struck in gold with a 1 D to indicate the value of one dollar and were the approximate size of a gold dollar. There is speculation that the 1 D dies may have been confiscated. This was also after 1933, the year President Franklin D. Roosevelt outlawed the ownership of gold by private

J3 - 1 ★ 10K SOLID GOLD 1939

citizens. A new variety, J3, evolved with the 10K SOLID GOLD as before with a 1 to the left, but the D to the right which represented Dollar was replaced with a five pointed star. All J3's are found with a medal orientation. Apparently the changes resolved Charbneau's problems with the Treasury as he continued to sell numerous varieties of his gold dollar souvenirs at the GGIE. The J3 is a great rarity with 10-20 likely surviving.

J4 - 1 ★ 22K SOLID GOLD 1939

The next variety to appear was the same gold dollar design, but the 10K was counterstamped 22K (J4). Perhaps customer's requests for a higher gold content motivated Charbneau. The planchet is the same diameter, but the weight increased significantly from 1.21 grams to 1.92 grams reflecting the higher gold content. The 22K counterstamped varieties are seldom encountered and the J4 has an estimated 5-10 surviving examples. This variety is found with both a coin and medal orientation.

The fair ended in October 1939 and reopened in May of 1940. Some of the 1939 1 D 10K Solid Gold (J2) varieties that were not sold were counterstamped with a "40" on the reverse for sale as souvenirs in 1940. The reverse "40" counterstamped variety is attributed as J5 and is one of the rarest Charbneau varieties with just 5-10 surviving examples.

J5 - 1 D 10K SOLID GOLD "40" 1939

All of Charbneau's gold dollars and only the gold dollars; not the silver, copper, or gold plated varieties; have the initials CMJ on the obverse in the hair of Pacifica. The reverse dies used for all Charbneau dollars are dated 1939 and 1940 and all are signed CMJ. Whomever CMJ is likely engraved the dies and Charbneau in all probability created the design as he had designed an earlier dollar-sized gold medal for the 1909 Alaska-Yukon-Pacific Exposition. Charbneau claimed the design efforts for the 1909 gold

The elongated Lincoln cent from the 1915 Panama Pacific International Exposition pictured here is signed CMJ along the lower edge of the exergue.

medal in his autobiography (appropriately published as a miniature book), but did not mention the 1939 effort. Burnie reported that he was unable to determine the identity of CMJ and some have suggested that they are Charbneau's initials reversed, a nom de-plume as it were. Jules L. Charbneau rules out his own initials. The initials CMJ appear on two elongated cents from the 1915 Panama Pacific International Exposition

The initials CMJ are approximately .5 mm high, the work of a master engraver. They are nearly obscured by the flow lines on the elongated cent on the left.

as well. Penny smashers produced and sold elongated cents at virtually every exposition as they proved to be popular souvenirs after their introduction at the 1893 Columbian exposition.

The fine detail work required to engrave dies for elongates and the Charbneau dollar was typically the work of jewelry engravers. A search of the years around 1915 in San Francisco city directories, the most likely location for someone engraving dies for use by penny smashers in San Francisco, reveals only one CMJ working as a jewelry engraver, a Carl M. Johnson. A second engraver, Charles M. Johnson proved to be a photo engraver, a far different profession and skill set. In any event, Carl M. Johnson, the jewelry engraver, was the only one still in business in 1939 and 1940. We believe Carl M. Johnson most likely engraved the Charbneau dies, although we cannot prove that with the information available today.

In addition to the five gold varieties, Charbneau produced three silver varieties for sale in 1939. On the obverse, the bust of Pacifica with the legend PACIFICA above remained the same, but the 1 and D or star have been removed and the SOLID GOLD notation has been replaced with STERLING (J6). An estimated 30-40 examples of the sterling J6 variety exist. All

sterling varieties weigh between 1.13 and 1.15 grams. Charbneau also sold a number of silver pieces which were gold-plated (J7). It is interesting to imagine Charbneau selling his customers a small souvenir medal with the legend STERLING that appears to be gold. The sterling gold-plated J7 are one of the more common Charbneau's with 30-50 estimated surviving.

J8 - STERLING "40" 1939

Another silver variety, J8, was created by counterstamping "40" on the reverse. Dated 1939, these souvenirs were also most likely left over, unsold stock that were counterstamped with 40 on the reverse for sales in 1940, just as the gold variety (J5) was created with a counterstamped "40" on the reverse. All counterstamped examples are considerably rare and the J8 is estimated to have 5-10 surviving examples.

J9 - COPPER 1939

Charbneau struck two copper varieties in 1939. The copper designs are unique in that

J10 - COPPER GOLD-PLATED 1939

there is no legend below Pacifica indicating either gold or sterling or in this case copper content. The fields for the copper pieces (J9) have a distinct orange peal roughness instead of the flat smooth fields that are found on all of the gold and silver varieties. Probably one of the greatest Charbneau rarities is the un-plated copper piece, J9, with likely 2-3 remaining. Charbneau also decided to gold plate some of the copper pieces so they are found in either plain copper or gold-plated copper (J10), both dated 1939. The gold-plated copper pieces J10 are probably the most common with 30-50 specimens existing.

J11 - 1 ★ 10K SOLID GOLD 1940

Ten varieties were produced for 1939, and only three varieties were produced for the year 1940, two in gold and one in silver. The first 1940 gold variety identified as J11 has the legend 10K SOLID GOLD as the previous 1939 dated gold varieties, but the planchet is considerably thinner and weighs 1.00 grams as opposed to the 1.21–1.22 grams of the heavier 1939 varieties. It is doubtful the public was aware of the lessened gold content of the 1940 dated gold varieties. Seldom encountered, the J11 probably has 5-10 surviving examples. All 1940 medals show evidence on the reverse of re-engraving the last two digits of the date 40 over 39.

J12 - 1 ★ 22K Solid Gold 1940

In 1940 Charbneau also produced a higher gold content variety as he did in 1939. J12 has 22 counterstamped over 10K similar to the J5 variety. The weight for the 1940 22K variety is heavier at 1.90 grams as would be expected and consistent with the weight of the 1939 22K varieties. Between 5-10 J12 varieties are estimated to exist.

Only one silver variety was produced in 1940 and no copper varieties are known. The silver variety J13 has STERLING below the bust and is dated 1940. No 1940 silver pieces were gold-plated or counterstamped as they

J13 - Sterling 1940

were in 1939. J13 has an estimated 20-30 examples surviving.

With an estimated population of between 150-300 examples, today Charbneau dollars are popular and rare enough to create some excitement when offered for sale as most So-Called Dollar collectors need at least one variety for their collection.

1939 Gold So-Called Dollars

J #	Date	Pacifica lower legend	Orientation	Weight in grams
J1	1939	1 D SOLID GOLD	Coin	1.22
J2	1939	1 D 10 K SOLID GOLD	Coin and Medal	1.22
J3	1939	1 ★ 10 K SOLID GOLD	Medal	1.21
J4	1939	1 ★ 22 (COUNTERSTAMPED OVER) 10K SOLID GOLD	Medal and Coin	1.92
J5	1939	1 D 10K SOLID GOLD 40 COUNTERSTAMPED ON REVERSE FIELD	Coin	1.22

J1 - 1 D Solid Gold 1939

1.22 GM · 12 MM · COIN ORIENTATION

GOLDEN GATE INT. EXPOSITION
1939

J2 - 1 D 10K Solid Gold 1939

1.22 GM · 12 MM · COIN AND MEDAL ORIENTATION

GOLDEN GATE INT. EXPOSITION
1939

J3 - 1 ★ 10K Solid Gold 1939

1.21 GM · 12 MM · MEDAL ORIENTATION

GOLDEN GATE INT. EXPOSITION
1939

J4 - 1 ★ 22K Solid Gold 1939

1.92 GM 12 MM MEDAL AND COIN ORIENTATION

GOLDEN GATE INT. EXPOSITION
1939

J5 - 1 D 10K Solid Gold "40" 1939

1.22 gm · 12 mm · Coin Orientation

GOLDEN GATE INT. EXPOSITION
40
1939

GOLDEN GATE INTERNATIONAL EXPOSITION
1939
SAN FRANCISCO
BAY

1939 Silver So-Called Dollars

J #	Date	Pacifica lower legend	Orientation	Weight in grams
J6	1939	sterling	Medal	1.14
J7	1939	Sterling (Gold-Plated)	Medal	1.14
J8	1939	1 sterling 40 counterstamped on reverse field	Medal	1.15

J6 - STERLING 1939

1.14 GM • 12 MM • MEDAL ORIENTATION

GOLDEN GATE INT. EXPOSITION
1939

J7 - STERLING GOLD-PLATED 1939

1.14 GM · 12 MM · MEDAL ORIENTATION

GOLDEN GATE INT. EXPOSITION
1939

J8 - Sterling "40" 1939

1.15 GM · 12 MM · Medal Orientation

GOLDEN GATE INT. EXPOSITION
40
1939

PACIFIC
GOLDEN GATE INT. EXPOSITION

GOLDEN GATE INT. EXP

1939 Copper So-Called Dollars

J #	Date	Pacifica lower legend	Orientation	Weight in grams
J9	1939	(blank)	Coin	0.92
J10	1939	(blank) (Gold-Plated)	Coin	0.95

J9 - Copper 1939

0.92 gm ● 12 mm ● Coin Orientation

GOLDEN GATE INT. EXPOSITION
1939

J10 - COPPER GOLD-PLATED 1939

0.95 GM · 12 MM · COIN ORIENTATION

GOLDEN GATE INT. EXPOSITION
1939

GOLDEN GATE INTERNATIONAL EXPOSITION
1940
SAN FRANCISCO
BAY

1940 Gold So-Called Dollars

J #	Date	Pacifica lower legend	Orientation	Weight in grams
J11	1940	1 ★ 10 K SOLID GOLD	Medal	1.00
J12	1940	1 ★ 22 (COUNTERSTAMPED OVER) 10K SOLID GOLD	Medal	1.90

J11 - 1 ★ 10K SOLID GOLD 1940

1.00 GM · 12 MM · MEDAL ORIENTATION

GOLDEN GATE INT. EXPOSITION
1940

J12 - 1 ★ 22K SOLID GOLD 1940

1.90 GM · 12 MM · MEDAL ORIENTATION

GOLDEN GATE
INT EXPOSITION

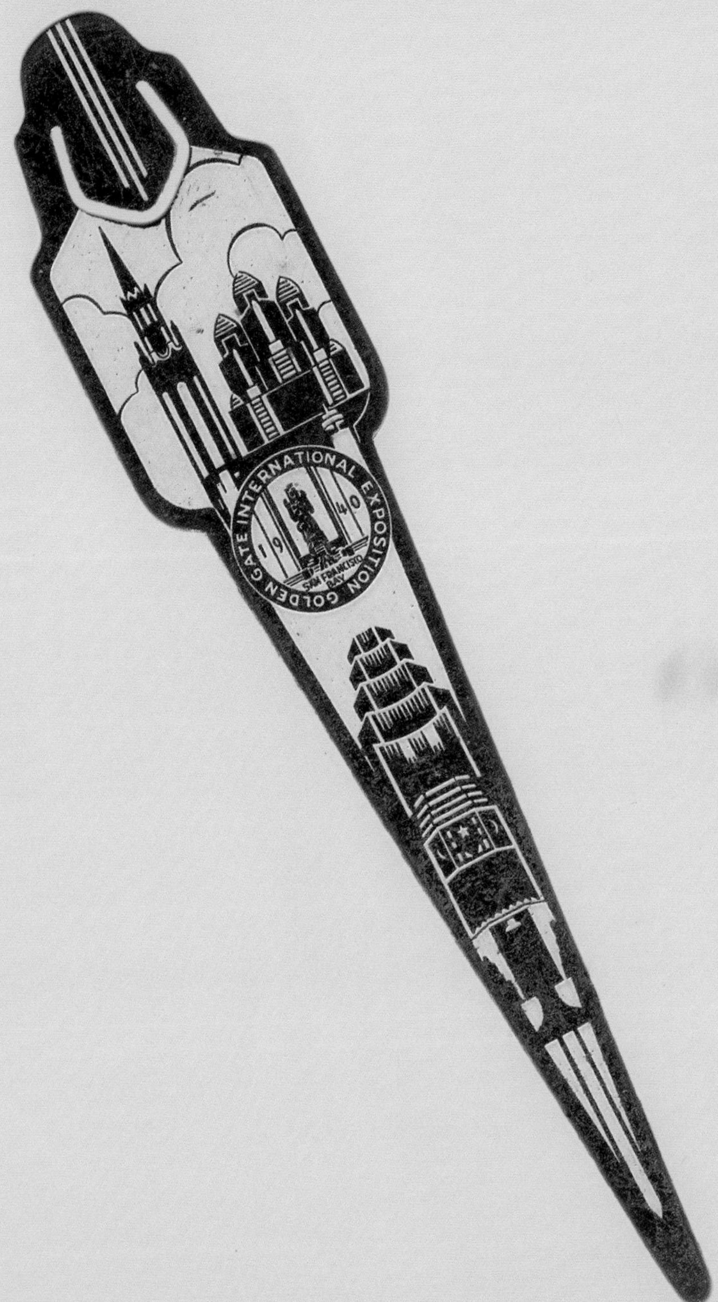
GOLDEN GATE INTERNATIONAL EXPOSITION
1940
SAN FRANCISCO BAY

1940 Silver So-Called Dollar

J #	Date	Pacifica lower legend	Orientation	Weight in grams
J13	1939	sterling	Coin	1.14

J13 - Sterling 1940

1.14 GM · 12 MM · COIN ORIENTATION

GOLDEN GATE INT. EXPOSITION
1940

JULES CHARBNEAU
643 STOCKTON ST.
SAN FRANCISCO, CALIF.
JULES CHARBNEAU
643 STOCKTON ST.
SAN FRANCISCO, CALIF.
PACIFICA
PACIFICA
PACIFICA

New Directions in Research

We began this project wanting to document the confirmed varieties of 1939 and 1940 Charbneau dollars and present them in a format that would enhance their appreciation. They are small—tiny—almost too tiny to fully appreciate. As our work progressed, other stories became entwined with that of Jules Charbneau. His choice of a gold souvenir dollar made more sense when we learned that he designed a souvenir dollar for the Alaska-Yukon-Pacific Exposition. But why was that gold piece attributed to M.E. Hart and the "Coins of the Golden West" as is commonly repeated in auction catalogs? To answer that question, we returned to Burnie's *Small California and Territorial Gold Coins* and that took us in directions we never imagined at the outset of our research.

Burnie explains in his introduction that he wished to share the information he gathered over the years collecting small California Gold coins, pioneer fractional gold as most choose to call them today. Just enough ambiguity exists in whether any of the pieces actually functioned as "coins" to lead many collectors to branch into the related small California gold charms and souvenirs. Jewelers and others continued to produce gold charms after the Treasury Department made it clear that only the U.S. government had the authority to coin money. It is only one more small step for collectors to include other examples of small gold tokens and souvenirs and these Burnie listed in a Supplement section that included territorial and state gold pieces (other than California) and other token or souvenir pieces, including the Charbneau dollars.

Among the token or souvenir pieces are those struck for various expositions including the Alaska-Yukon-Pacific Exposition, the Lewis and Clark Exposition, the Panama Pacific International Exposition, and the Golden Gate International Exposition (the Charbneau so-called dollar). Burnie lists nine Charbneau varieties (see concordance table), only three of which are included in our survey. The other six listed by Burnie are either incorrectly described or based on misinformation.

Hibler and Kappen list four types in their 1963 edition of *So-Called Dollars*, but the 2008 second edition includes more detail allowing for eight varieties and up to 10 subtypes of the gold varieties depending on how one interprets the textual descriptions.

Weber tried to make sense of the possible eighteen varieties suggested by Burnie and Hibler and Kappen in a 2002

Concordance Table

Our thirteen types compared with those listed in Burnie, Hibler and Kappen, and Weber. We are using the numbering system from the second edition of H&K. Numbers are repeated for some entries as H&K list the general description that gold pieces may have 1 D or 1★. Weber states that the platinum pieces listed by Hibler and Kappen were struck with the J1 die, but Hibler and Kappen provide no description for the platinum pieces if they do exist. Burnie does not describe 1★gold pieces and he does not provide a source for the 14 K designation. It has been suggested that Bullowa's October 1949 auction is the source of the 14 K attribution, but Bullowa lists only the Solid Gold, 10 K, 22 K, and Sterling varieties .

J #	Date	Pacifica Lower Legend	Additional Information	Burnie #	Weber #	HK #
J1	1939	1 D SOLID GOLD		D 10	#6	HK 488
J2	1939	1 D 10 K SOLID GOLD		D 11	#7	HK 488
J3	1939	1 * 10K SOLID GOLD		UNLISTED	#8	HK 488
J4	1939	1 * 22 (C/S OVER) 10K SOLID GOLD		UNLISTED	UNLISTED	HK 488
J5	1939	1 D 10K SOLID GOLD	40 COUNTER STAMPED ON REVERSE FIELD	D 14	#11	UNLISTED
J6	1939	STERLING		D10	#2	HK 487
J7	1939	STERLING	GOLD-PLATED	UNLISTED	#5	HK 487C
J8	1939	STERLING	40 COUNTER STAMPED ON REVERSE FIELD	UNLISTED	#3	HK 487B
J9	1939	(BLANK)	STIPPLED FIELDS, STRUCK IN COPPER	UNLISTED	UNLISTED	UNLISTED
J10	1939	(BLANK)	STIPPLED FIELDS, STRUCK IN COPPER, GOLD-PLATED	UNLISTED	#1	HK 490
J11	1940	1 * 10 K SOLID GOLD	THIN PLANCHET	UNLISTED	#14	HK 489
J12	1940	1 * 22 (C/S OVER) 10K SOLID GOLD		UNLISTED	#17	HK 489
J13	1940	STERLING		UNLISTED	#4	HK 487A
—	1939		PLATINUM	UNLISTED	#18	HK 1033
—	1939		1 D 14 K	D 12	#9	UNLISTED
—	1939		1 D 22 K	D 13	#10	UNLISTED
—	1940		1 D SOLID GOLD	D 15	#12	UNLISTED
—	1940		1 D 10 K	D 16	#13	UNLISTED
—	1940		1 D 14 K	D 17	#15	UNLISTED
—	1940		1 D 22 K	D 18	#16	UNLISTED

summary article published by the Pacific Coast Numismatic Society. While Weber's descriptions are the easiest to follow, he ultimately repeats misinformation present in the literature of the time. Our concordance table aligns the actual pieces we have examined and photographed with the previous listings.

While our research focused on the Golden Gate International Exposition, we could not ignore our discovery that Jules Charbneau had executed an earlier design for an Alaskan-Yukon-Pacific Exposition gold souvenir. The one pennyweight version of Charbneau's gold three token series is collected as a so-called dollar, so we were familiar with it. Hibler and Kappen, however, describe it as being issued by M. E. Hart Co. of San Francisco, who they describe as "sponsors of many gold issues between 1908 and 1915." Although Burnie is not listed among their acknowledgements or references, it is clear that the attribution to M. E. Hart can be traced to Burnie.

Burnie likely included the "Small Territorial and State Gold" issues because he owned one of the copper-framed sets from the Panama Pacific International Exposition with the title, "Coins of the Golden West." The name of the firm—M. E. Hart & Co., 560 Powell St., San Francisco—on a printed card was attached to the back of the frame. Burnie begins the section with the statement that he believed "these were the forerunners of the rather prolific series, and paved the way for the issuance of the other varieties."

Our efforts to learn more about the man, Jules Charbneau, opened an unexpected door in our research efforts. Did M. E. Hart make the gold tokens that Charbneau designed? Why would Charbneau look to San Francisco to find someone to execute his designs when there were token and medal manufactures in Seattle?

We suspected that M. E. Hart did not make the 1909 A.Y.P.E. gold pieces even though Hart sold them at a later date. One cannot deny that the existence of the framed set of gold tokens associated with M. E. Hart and an advertising card showing the A.Y.P.E. tokens among others is strong evidence linking Hart to the series. Nevertheless, we had the evidence of Charbneau's design patent and newspaper reports that he was selling the three token sets through Ye Olde Curiosity Shop as early as February 1909, and that suggests that Hart might not be the actual maker of the tokens.

Despite the fact that the souvenir tokens, in particular the A.Y.P.E. tokens, are invariably described as being made by M. E. Hart, Burnie does conclude that Hart "did not manufacture any of the coins or souvenirs they offered, but instead procured them from the manufacturers of them." Two brief announcements in 1916 magazines confirm that M. E. Hart was buying left over stock of some medals and gold coins, specifically mint struck medals from the 1916 Panama-California Exposition in San Diego and commemorative gold dollars struck by the U.S. Mint for the 1915 Panama Pacific International Exposition. The latter pieces honoring labor could be purchased for $2.25 or $2.75 when mounted as a charm, stickpin, or brooch pin.

So who was M. E. Hart and what was the connection with the gold series and expositions? A search of San Francisco city directories narrowed the choice to a Mary E. Hart, a widow, and Morton E. Hart, an audiologist. Morton Hart seemed to be the most likely candidate since his place of business was in the 200 block of Powell, just three blocks from the location of M. E. Hart & Co. But, why would an audiologist run a second business from another location to sell stock remainders from other manufacturers? Neither Hart was otherwise associated with the 560 Powell address.

Jules Charbneau surprised us at several turns in researching his personal history. We have been unable to make a direct personal link between him and Farran Zerbe, but their paths certainly crossed in St. Louis and Charbneau's A.Y.P.E. gold pieces seem to be influenced by Zerbe's gold tokens. Image our surprise when the name, Mary E. Hart, showed up in reviewing A.Y.P.E. literature. Could she be the mysterious M. E. Hart and if so, what could she have to do with the "Coins of the Golden West?" A lot it turned out.

Mary E. Hart is a common name, so it took some careful research to be certain we were tracking the correct individual through a variety of historical sources. She first appears in newspaper citations in 1893 as the editor and owner of the San Francisco women's literary magazine, *Pacific Monthly* (not to be confused with the later Portland-based *Pacific Monthly* that became *Sunset*). While the articles are unclear as to how she became owner, it seems she may have inherited her ownership. In 1893, she also assumes responsibility for Southern California historical collections displayed in the California Building at the 1893

Columbian Exposition. Without knowing much of her earlier history, we can note that she is a woman of letters and science as she was also serving as the secretary for the California Academy of Sciences.

A few years later, Hart travels to Alaska and works alongside men in the gold fields, successfully staking a number of claims in the area around Nome. She does more than prospect however and founds the Women's Club of Nome and becomes secretary of the Alaska Academy of Sciences. While there are few details into the exact nature of her businesses, Mary E. Hart establishes residences in Nome, San Francisco, and Corte Madera while maintaining active involvement in Nome and San Francisco society. Her trips between California and San Francisco often include a layover in Tacoma, Washington at the home of her brother-in-law, Louis F. Hart who later served as the lieutenant governor and then governor of Washington.

Although they had never met, the Interior Department's governor of the District of Alaska asked Mary E. Hart to organize and serve as the manager of Alaska's exhibits at the 1904 Louisiana Purchase Exposition in St. Louis where she was awarded a gold medal for her personal collection of Alaskan gold nuggets. While we cannot say that Mary E. Hart, Jules Charbneau, and Farran Zerbe ever met at that time, we find it interesting that all three individuals apparently involved with small gold tokens crossed paths in St. Louis.

Hart continued her travels between San Francisco and Alaska over the next few years and served as a travel lecturer on the Pacific Coast Steamship Company's steamer, Spokane. The 1909 A.Y.P.E. drew her back to Washington and she served as the Alaska women's commissioner to the exposition, organizing Alaskan exhibits for the exposition. Again, we cannot demonstrate that she met Charbneau, but his father-in-law also worked with those arranging the Alaskan exhibits and exhibited his own collection of Alaska ivory artifacts. It would surprise us if Mary and Joseph did not meet in 1909 since both worked on the Alaskan exhibits. They may in fact have met much earlier since their collecting interests overlapped in Alaska. Given the fame of Ye Olde Curiosity Shop, we find it hard to believe that Mary E. Hart would pass through the Seattle port on numerous trips and never once visit the popular store.

Her journeys between Alaska and San Francisco continued after the fair, both to manage her business interests in Alaska and promote Pacific Coast Steamship tours as well as to collect items for exhibit at the planned 1915 Panama Pacific International Exposition. For the latter activities, she met with members of the Alaska Cruiser's Club of California near the apartment she maintained at Union Square. While we cannot positively say that M. E. Hart & Co. of 560 Powell St. and Mary E. Hart are one and the same, the proximity of her choice of residence in San Francisco and the location of the company address seem too close to be a lucky coincidence.

Assuming M. E. Hart and Mary E. Hart are one and the same, that would mean she was selling small gold souvenirs, individually and in sets known as the "Coins of the Golden West" through Farran Zerbe at the 1915 exposition. The sets include the Charbneau A.Y.P.E. gold pieces that must have been acquired from Charbneau or, more likely, his father-in-law at Ye Olde Curiosity Shop in Seattle.

So-called dollar enthusiasts and exposition collectors actively collect Charbneau dollars and the dollars are frequently listed with California pioneer fractional gold and small factional gold pieces of the American west. When we began our research, Charbneau dollars, in our opinion, were a unique expression of a man who specialized in the world of high quality miniatures made to exact detail. His souvenir medals were one expression of his specialty that visitors could share and take home.

We now know that he likely did intend the "D" in "1 D" to be interpreted as a dollar. Charbneau himself likely called them coins in his conversations with the public. Our research suggests that the Charbneau dollar was likely conceived as an expression of the western tradition of producing small, fractional gold pieces, although we cannot definitively prove the connections between Charbneau, Farran Zerbe, and Mary E. Hart proposed here. That awaits further research.

Bibliography

Newspaper Articles

—
"Alaska Women's Share in the Fair," University of Washington Libraries, Special Collections, Collection 979.7432 Alaska Yukon Pacific Exposition, newspaper clipping, ca. 1908.

—
"Artists Rap Fair Tower, 'Better a Grain Elevator'," *San Francisco Chronicle*, December 22, 1938, p. 7.

—
"Charbneau Day to be Celebrated," *Oakland Tribune*, October 19, 1939, p. 16.

—
"Magazines," *Los Angeles Times*, May 8, 1890, p. 4.

—
"He Makes Pretty A.-Y.-P. Souvenir Gold Coins," *The Star*, February 13, 1909, p. 3.

—
"Mr. Connick to Exposition Critics: Statues Just Nazi, Wide and Thick, Mostly Thick, Especially From Rear," *San Francisco Chronicle*, December 23, 1938, p. 11.

—
"Mrs. Mary E. Hart Will Represent Alaska at St. Louis," *San Francisco Call*, January 8, 1904, p. 11.

—
"Pirate Queens to Rule Fair, Yerba Buena Site Will Be Named 'Treasure Island'," *San Francisco Chronicle*, February 19, 1937, p. 16.

—
"She Goes from Tacoma in Far North to Collect Great Set of Curios for the Fair," *Tacoma Times*, March 10, 1914, p. 5.

—
"Thousands of Souvenirs to Flood Nation With Trade Marks of Treasure Island," *San Francisco Chronicle*, February 1, 1939, p. 7.

—
"Two Chairs and a Table on the Head of a Pin!," *San Francisco Chronicle*, February 10, 1939, p. 17.

—
"Western States Atomic Vaults Inc. Will Open Today," *Santa Cruz Sentinel*, May 2, 1954.

—
"Woman Pioneer of Alaska Dies," *Los Angeles Times*, March 10, 1921, p. 115.

—
"Woman to Gather Alaska Exhibit," University of Washington Libraries, Special Collections, Collection 979.7432 Alaska Yukon Pacific Exposition, newspaper clipping, ca. 1908.

Burroughs, Jack
"Art Rampant in Portugal Pavilion, Hoofaloger Finds," *Oakland Tribune*, April 25, 1939, p. 19.

"Tower and Court Glimpses of Fair," *Oakland Tribune*, March 22, 1939, p. 14.

"Hoofaloger is Now Exhibit," *Oakland Tribune*, June 25, 1939, p. 14.

"Tower and Court - - -," *Oakland Tribune*, March 7, 1939, p. 14.

Caen, Herb
"It's News to Me," *San Francisco Chronicle*, December 21, 1940, p. 11.

Silverman, Jan
"It's a Small World for Collector of Miniatures," *Oakland Tribune People*, April 2, 1976. Pp. 19, 21.

Books and Journal Articles

—
"1916 San Diego Exposition Medal," *The Numismatist,* 29(6): 258, 1916.

—
Official Guide Book: Golden Gate International Exposi-

tion on San Francisco Bay, San Francisco: Crocker Co., 1939.

—

Official guide to the Alaska-Yukon-Pacific Exposition: Seattle, Washington, June 1 to October 16, 1909, Seattle: Alaska-Yukon-Pacific Exposition Pub. Co., 1909.

—

"Recent Publications," *Miniature Book News*, 14:6, 1968.

—

"The Man on the Wall," *The Bricklayer, Mason and Plasterer*, 19(10):211, 1916.

—

"They're Tiny – But They Work," *Popular Mechanics*, 74(6): 856-859, 1940.

Atlass, Beatrice (editor)
Radio City Music Hall Weekly, 2:40, 1937.

Bullowa, David M.
Catalog of Rare American, Ancient and Foreign Coins, etc., Philadelphia: Auction Catalog, October 7, 8 1949.

Burnie, R. H.
Small California and Territorial Gold Coins, Quarter Dollars, Half Dollars, Dollars, Pascagoula, MS, 1955.

Charbneau, Jules
Jules Charbneau's World of Miniatures, Wenatchee, WA: Privately Published by Isabella Charbneau Warren, 1968.

Duncan, Kate
1001 Curious Things: Ye Olde Curiosity Shop and Native American Art, Seattle: University of Washington Press, 2000.

Harris, Audrey E.
"The Charbneau Collection," *Nutshell News* 17(9): 52-54, 1987.

Hibler, Harold E. and Charles V. Kappen
So-Called Dollars; An Illustrated Standard Catalog, Clifton, N.J.:Coin and Currency Institute, 1963. Second Edition, 2008.

James, Jack and Earle Weller
Treasure Island, "The Magic City", 1939-1940: The Story of the Golden Gate International Exposition, San Francisco: Pisani Printing and Publishing Co., 1941.

Kenney, Richard D.
"So-Called Dollars: Exposition and Commemorative Medals, Bryan and Lesher Dollars, Miscellaneous Monetary and Other Issues," *The Coin Collector's Journal* 20(4): 1-20, July-August 1953.

Maloney, Russell and Helen Cooke
"The Talk of the Town, Tiny Collection," *New Yorker*, July 24, 1937, pp. 10-12.

Okrent, Daniel
Great Fortune: The Epic of Rockefeller Center, New York: Viking, 2003.

Rydell, Robert W., John E. Findling, and Kimberly D. Pelle
Fair America: World's Fairs in the United States, Washington, D.C.: Smithsonian Books, 2000.

Shevlin, Jeff
"The Bill Weber Collection of So-Called Dollars and $50 Slug Facsimiles," *Holabird-Kagin Americana Auctions Auction #2*. Reno, 2008.

Smith, James R.
San Francisco's Lost Landmarks, Fresno: Word Dancer Press, 2005.

Weber, Bill
"The Charbneau dollars of the Golden Gate International Exposition," *Collected Papers*, San Francisco: Pacific Coast Numismatic Society, pp. 59-63. 2002.

ACKNOWLEDGEMENTS

The authors appreciate the assistance they received from collectors, dealers, and institutions while researching and producing *Charbneau So-Called Dollars*. Collectors Randy Clark, Jim Vanek, Robert Rhue, Michael Wehner, and Jerry Schimmel shared data from their collections, personal observations from their combined years of numismatic experience, and made items available for study and photography. Fred Holabird provided the opportunity to catalog Bill Weber's collection of Charbneau so-called dollars. Elizabeth Hahn, American Numismatic Society Librarian located and copied material in response to our inquiries. The library of the American Numismatic Association was an invaluable asset, ready to lend materials to supplement our personal libraries. The University of California Santa Cruz library provided access to newspapers files and other archival material. Debra Kaufman at the California Historical Society assisted with locating materials and records in the society's library. Carolyn Marr, Librarian at the Seattle Museum of History and Industry went out of her way to find materials that were helpful in expanding our research.

Special thanks are due to Todd Pollack for his excellent, detailed photographs of the exceptionally small medals. His work facilitated our examination and comparison of individual medals. We are honored that D. Wayne "Dick" Johnson agreed to contibute the Preface for our work.

We want to thank the dealers who helped support the costs of publishing this work to help keep the costs within reason for collectors. Their institutional advertisements are found in the last pages.

Finally, we want to acknowledge the value we receive from the organizations that serve collectors of so-called dollars including the American Numismatic Association, the Token and Medal Society, and the National Token Collector's Association.

Thank you all.

Jeff Shevlin
William D. Hyder

About the Authors

Jeff Shevlin:

Jeff is a writer, researcher, publisher, cataloger, public speaker, dealer, and numismatic consultant to major auction firms on So-Called Dollars. A life member of the ANA, he is also an instructor at the Summer Seminar hosted by the ANA. Jeff is preparing a new standard catalog of So-Called Dollars and is actively engaging the numismatic community in his research. Jeff has written numerous articles, given over 50 presentations and developed dozens of award winning competitive exhibits. Jeff served as the General Chairman for the 2011 National Money Show in Sacramento in 2011 and was the Numismatic Theatre Chairman in 1999. He is a former publisher of *The California Numismatist*, the official publication of the California State Numismatic Association (CSNA) and the Numismatic Association of Southern California. He has been an officer of numerous coin clubs including the CSNA, the Sacramento Valley Coin Club, and the Civil War Token Society. Jeff cataloged the "Bill Weber So-Called Dollar Auction" for Holabird-Kagin Americana which received the Numismatic Literary Guild (NLG) 2009 Award of Extraordinary Merit for the Best Auction Catalog Exonumia.

William D. Hyder:

Bill has collected coins for more than 45 years and is a frequent contributor to *The Numismatist* and *TAMS Journal*. His collecting interests include Celtic and Roman coins of Gaul and Spain, medieval French coins, French jetons, early American tokens, so-called dollars, and medals. In addition to his numismatic interests, he is a specialist in the archaeology of prehistoric art with an emphasis on the American West and Southwest. He is co-author of the *Medallic Portraits of Adolf Hitler* with R. W. Colbert. His writings have earned the 1981 TAMS Mishler Exonumia Cataloging Award, the 1986 ANA Silver (Second Place) Heath Literary Award, and the 2010 TAMS David Schenkman Gold Literary Award. He is a past president of the Santa Barbara Coin Club and is currently secretary of the Pacific Coast Numismatic Society and webmaster for the Token and Medal Society.

Book Designed by

William D. Hyder
Datura Press
Scotts, Valley, California

Photography by:

Todd Pollock
Jeff Shevlin
William D. Hyder

Holabird-Kagin Americana
3555 Airway Drive #308, Reno, NV 89511
(775) 852-8822 Toll-Free: (877) 852-8822
www.holabirdamericana.com
Rediscovering History ~ Remembering Legends ~ Collecting the West
PURVEYORS OF FINE ORIGINAL
WESTERN AMERICANA & NUMISMATICS
* Ingots * Gold * Silver * Tokens * Coins * So-Called Dollars
*Historical Documents * Ephemera* Photographs * Bottles * More! *
HOLABIRD-KAGIN AMERICANA PRESENTS
BILL WEBER
SO CALLED DOLLARS
LIVE AUCTION - TUESDAY DECEMBER 2, 2008
Flip Catalog to view HKA Auction #2!
*Award winning catalog & record breaking sale for the
Bill Weber Collection of So-Called Dollars
December 2008

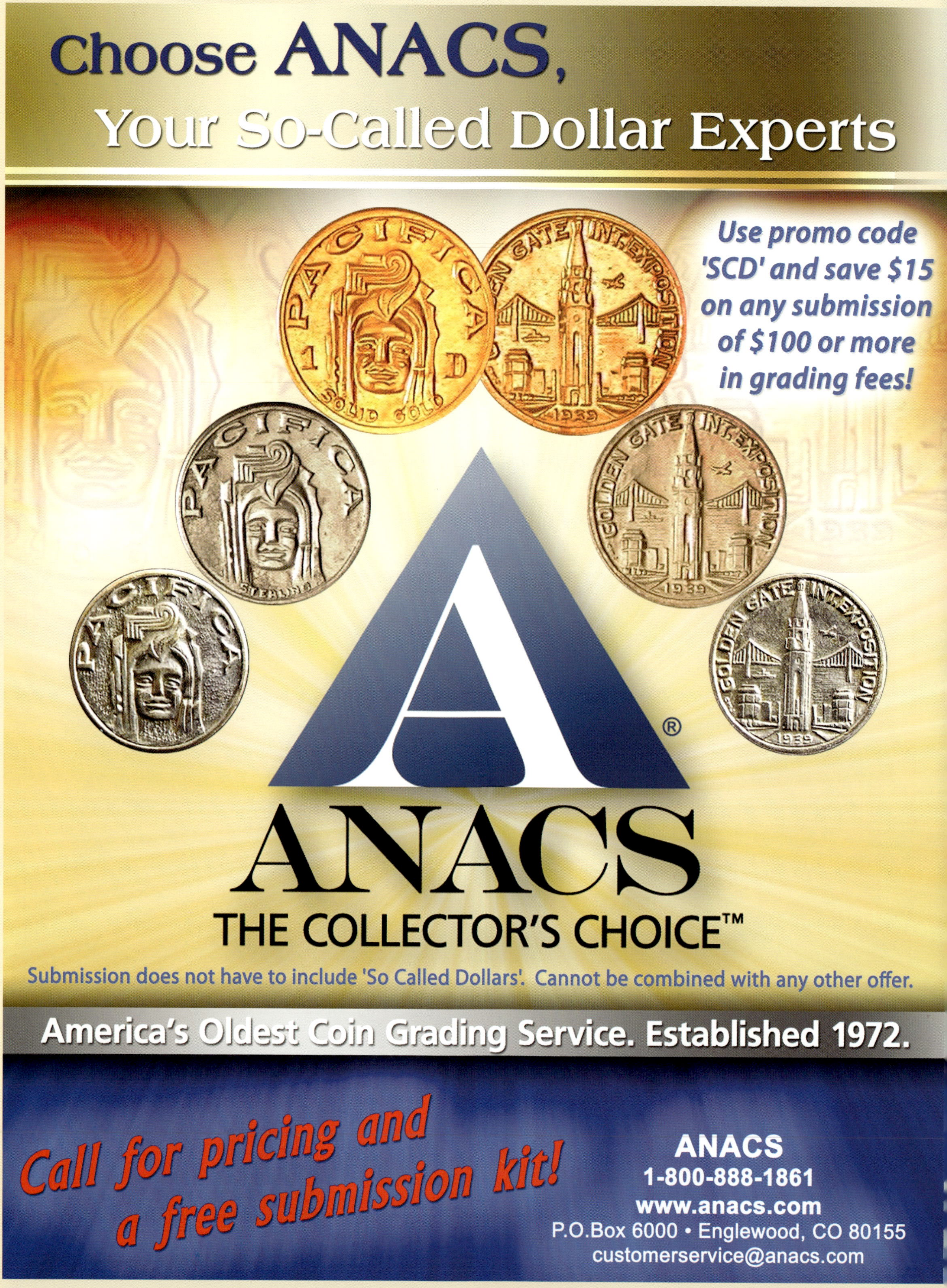
Choose ANACS,
Your So-Called Dollar Experts
Use promo code 'SCD' and save $15 on any submission of $100 or more in grading fees!
PACIFICA
1 D
SOLID GOLD
GOLDEN GATE INT. EXPOSITION
1939
STERLING
ANACS
THE COLLECTOR'S CHOICE™
Submission does not have to include 'So Called Dollars'. Cannot be combined with any other offer.
America's Oldest Coin Grading Service. Established 1972.
Call for pricing and a free submission kit!
ANACS
1-800-888-1861
www.anacs.com
P.O.Box 6000 • Englewood, CO 80155
customerservice@anacs.com